PUMPS WITH HOLES IN

Childhood Memoirs

David A Prosser

en Press

First published in Great Britain by Pen Press

ISBN: 978-1-78003-014-2

Pen Press is an imprint of
Indepenpress Publishing Ltd
25 Eastern Place
Brighton
BN2 1GJ

Printed and bound in the UK

This book was written for my three children,

Anthony, Wendy and Matthew

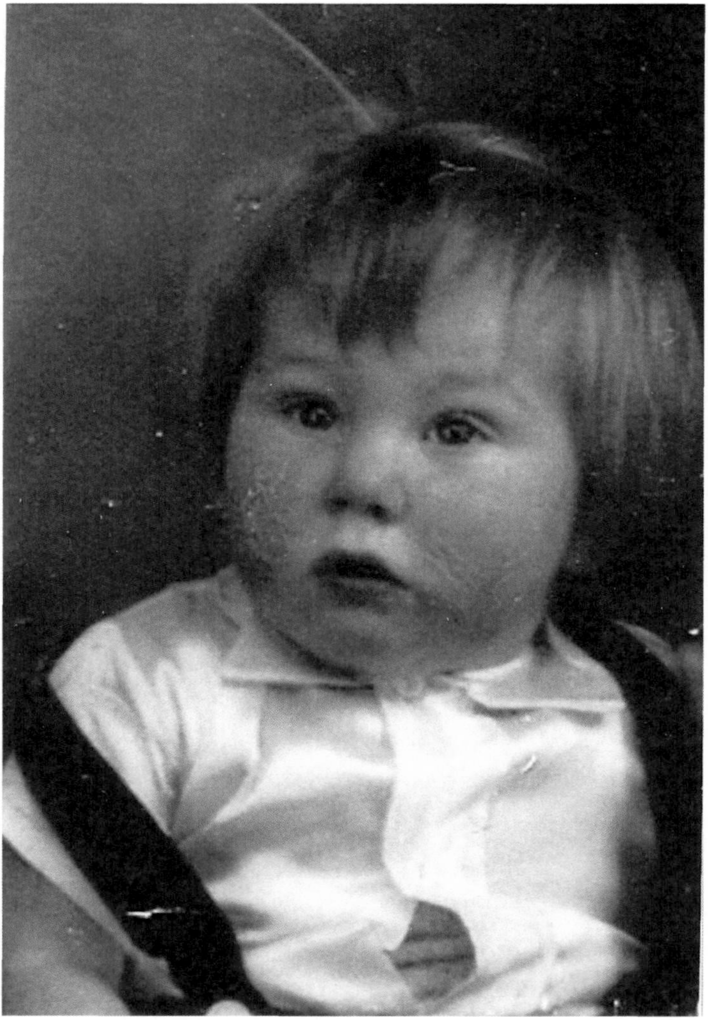

The author at the tender age of eighteen months
(born 30th October 1943)

I dedicate this book
to my lifelong friend

Trevor Kendall

You were five and I was four
I went to your house and knocked on your door
That was the first time we ever met
A life of friendship I will never regret
We ran errands even carried coal
No shoes had we, only pumps with holes.
Our memories are strong even though we are old.

The author with his sisters.
left to right: Kathleen, Janet, Doreen

ACKNOWLEDGEMENTS

My grateful thanks go to my ex-wife Irene for patiently going through this book page by page correcting my spelling mistakes, of which there were many. When my memory needed a nudge she was there to remind me, because I had told her that many times about my childhood – she had endured them from the tender age of sixteen when we first met on 13th March 1960 – she knows my childhood better than me. I owe it to her for encouraging me to sit down and write about my colourful childhood.

Putting together memoirs of my childhood brings back so many memories and images, not always good ones but fondly remembered; the ones I have compiled in this book are the ones most vivid in my memory. There are, of course, many more but the ones I have written about I think are the most interesting to read about.

My grateful thanks to the two artists
for the line drawings they did

Mr Alan Waite
and
Mr Graham Wilson

ABOUT THE AUTHOR

David was a real Brummie born to a very loving mother. His family lived in a council house in the Stechford area of Birmingham, where nearby there were fields, trees to climb, a river to play in and lots of places to explore.

He spent 1948 to 1958 at Audley Road School being very sporty, playing in goal at football and representing the school all through his school days and he excelled at high jumping.

As a young boy, known as Pross to all his friends, he had a poor but very colourful childhood. His life was filled with many adventures that hopefully you will enjoy reading about.

(Comments from a friend)

CONTENTS

Photos and Illustrations

YOUR LIFE

What makes life worthwhile?

As children we think that having lots of toys is the ultimate in life, having lots of cuddles, being told you are nice, sitting with your family, walking together down a country lane, seeing Mother Nature, looking at the trees, seeing the birds and knowing their names, learning to tell one from the other. To sit by a river and hear the sound of rippling water and feel the sun gently warming your back, to laugh and smile with your friends, to be with loved ones, to sit quietly sometimes and think how lucky you are.

The ultimate in life is to be told I love you, and for you to tell people you love them. These things in life cost nothing but fills the whole of your life with all the gifts you will ever need.

Plowden Road
(showing author's house, last one on the right)

Showing the bottom of Plowden Road
where it meets Swancote Road

INTRODUCTION

I WAS BORN IN THE YEAR 1943, October 30th, at 38 Plowden Road, Glebe Farm, Birmingham 33. My Mother being Dora Louisa Prosser (nee King), and Dad was William John Prosser, who everyone knew as Jack or Snowy.

We were a family of six; my two eldest brothers were in the forces so I rarely saw them, then they got married. So growing up until the age of five there were only four of us – me and my three sisters Kathleen, Doreen and Janet. My younger brother John was born five years after me.

My young life was surrounded by poverty and hardship, but after saying that it bred into me a sense of 'make do and mend and survival', with a mother so loving and caring she always put us first before herself, and a dad who mostly thought of himself (the majority of his money went on drink so he created the hardship we suffered). Our house consisted of three bedrooms upstairs, a living room, in the kitchen was a pantry, bathroom, coal hole, a cubby hole under the stairs and a cupboard next to the bathroom. There was an outside toilet, and a Belfast sink in the kitchen where Mother sat me as a child and bathed me more times than I remember. There was a wooden draining board that rested on the sink, and under the draining board was a boiler where Mom boiled up the water for us to have a bath – if on that Saturday or Sunday evening she had three spare pennies for the gas meter, if not we had no bath just a wash-down.

I was a little terror. I often had cuts and broken bones and my mom had several names for me, most of which I can't repeat. When I was born until the age of two I was known as 'grisle arse'. I cried so much and moaned so much my mom had to feed me continually (my wife said I haven't changed!). Most children have one bottle at feed time, I always had two and my sister Janet who is eighteen months older than me was always hungry. My mom couldn't understand why this was, until one day she saw me taking Janet's bottle from her and drinking it all.

As I was born two years before the end of the war, poverty for our family was there in all its glory, Dad being unemployed before the war. It was taking my parents a long time to recover in the post war years so everything was make do and mend, meaning my life and my sisters' did not improve for many years. Mother, bless her, could do wonders with six pence. Buying spuds for 1d (one penny) veggies 2d, and 2d worth of bones from the butcher's – I had to say, "for the dog", which we never had – she fed us for days.

I adored playing football, hopscotch, skipping, running, tip cat, table tennis and any games going. At the age of four and a half, I was playing with about six girls, as there were no boys living by me at that time.

MY LIFELONG FRIEND

One afternoon (I was coming up to my fifth birthday) I was sitting in the middle of the road opposite my front garden gate, drawing on the concrete road. I remember drawing a matchstick girl with a skirt on. My two sisters Doreen and Janet were playing with Ann Hill from across the road and the two girls from next door Beryle and Jacqueline Farrington, when I saw a lady walking down the road with a little boy:

"Who is the lady?" I asked my sister.

"They're moving into that empty house there," she said, pointing over the road.

The next day I knocked on the door and asked if the little boy could come out and play. That was very start of a life long friendship. We did a lot together from tatting, taking coach journeys, carrying coal, running errands, gardening and many, many more crazy things, we really enjoyed our childhood in spite of the poverty we grew up in.

His name is Trevor Kendall.

My Mom (on the left) with her best friend Lizzie (Trevor's mum)

Audley Road Secondary Modern School

Showing the entrance from Swancote Road, to the Infants and Juniors School Playgrounds. At the age of five, on my very first day of starting school, I walked up this entrance with my mom, across the Juniors' playground, through the tunnel to the Infants' playground.

This was the Infants' playground.
This tunnel is where my mom stood and watched me on my first day at school in 1948

This was the entrance I had to use when I went into the Senior School

This was my first classroom on my first day at school.

This wooden hut was two classrooms. On the right was the Infants, on the left the Juniors. I was in both those classrooms which have now been demolished.

2oz OF SWEETS

My earliest memory is when I was three years old. I used to stand on the window sill to watch the children coming out of school; I climbed on the chair, then the table, to get to the sill. Mom always told me off for climbing but she never took me off there, and I did it every day.

The school entrance was half way up Swancote Road, just a bit further up were our local shops and I went every day to the shops with my mom because we were quite poor. I rarely got sweets. One day I was playing my face (as my mom put it) for some sweets; Mom bought me 2oz of sweets, "Now don't tell your sisters you've had sweets." Being very greedy I ate them very quickly. As Mom was putting dinner on the table my sister Doreen walked in, I immediately said, "I haven't had any sweets have I? Mom." "Yes you have or you wouldn't have said that," said Doreen, then she played her face something awful till Mom gave her a good hiding with a smacked bum. I was told I wouldn't be given any sweets again, nor did I for a very long time.

It was a long time after that little episode, three years I bet it was, Mom bought some sweets and shared them between me and my two sisters. I thought, I will wait for them to finish theirs then I will start to eat mine; it was killing me not to eat mine, then when they had finished theirs I put a sweet in my mouth and made a sucking noise and saying, "Mmm, these are nice." Doreen shouted, "Mom, he is playing us up with his sweets because we have eaten ours!" "I know, I heard him," said Mom, so with a smack across the back of my head, my sweets were shared between my two sisters and I ended up with nothing. Well I cried my little heart out, but I never did it again – once bitten as the saying goes.

DROPS

Once a week my mom took me to a welfare clinic, which was situated an area called Kitts Green; I was three years old my mom told me some years later.

What I do remember, the first time I went to that clinic, was that I had drops down my ears, throat and up my nose and in my eyes. I've no idea what was wrong with me. After I screamed and fought like life depended on it they said, "If you're good you can have a bottle of this orange juice," smacking her lips to show me how nice it was. I was sold, that bribe worked every time (I always was thick). Unknown to me she always gave mom a bottle of Cod Liver Oil which she hid away from me, and I was held down at home to be given a spoonful of that (they would have to hold me down these days as well!). After, I was always given a spoonful of orange juice straight away, I loved that welfare orange juice – it was thick and sweet.

Mom's friend Winnie called at our house one morning. Mom said, "Come on, son, we're going for a walk." That excited me, and as we were walking I would keep asking, "Where are we going?" She would say, "Just for a walk, son." As we turned the corner I saw the bridge, I then knew what was on the other side of that bridge – the welfare clinic. Hurt and pain lay the other side of that bridge.

I pulled, shouted, cried very loudly, if I could have got free of Mom's grip I would have run off. I was what these days is known as 'throwing a wobbly', "Please, Mommy," I was saying, "Don't take me in there." Every time I saw that bridge I threw a wobbly, even to this very day when I see that bridge I get a horrible feeling in the pit of my stomach; those feelings do not seem to want to leave me.

Mothers then used to get baby food called National Dried Milk free for their children. I don't think in those days there was an air raid shelter, shed, coalhouse or pantry that hadn't got a National Dried Milk tin in there – I've seen them with nails, screws, tools, drills, car bits, motor bike bits, you name it those tins housed it. We had a couple of those tins in our house, I was informed by my better half. National Dried Milk full cream was a silver tin then later white with blue writing. Half cream was silver and again later white with red writing. I have even seen those tins made into toys. I've seen lorry and a train, I bet there are hundreds still out there in the shape of every toy you can think of (I want one!).

The dreaded bridge to the Welfare Clinic

The Welfare Clinic as it was at that time.

SHORT BACK AND SIDES

The first time I went to the barbers I didn't go to school then as I was only four and a half years old. Mom took me for a hair cut known as short back and sides, the name of the barbers was Tranters, he was our local barber. As Mom walked in with me Mr Tranter said, "Leave him here while you do your shopping." I said, "I don't want my hair cut, Mom." "You'll be OK, son," she said, so off she went shopping.

Well he fought with me to get me into that chair; just when he thought he had won he was puffing and blowing, I jumped out of that chair and ran into the street outside to find my mom. He came running after me caught hold of my arm so I kicked him as hard as I could – I cannot print what he said to me! He dragged me back inside, threw me into the chair and I mean threw, I must have bounced about two foot into the air. With a very loud voice he yelled down my ear, "Now sit still," so I did because he scared me. Comb and scissors no problem – I remember thinking, this is all right, then he turned the electric clippers on and started to shave by my ear. I flew out of that chair, ducked under his arms and ran outside with the sheet still wrapped around me. He got hold of me, so I kicked him again, he shook me and dragged me back into the shop, he was much rougher with me that time than the time before, again I was thrown back into that chair. I think I bounced four foot that second time; he only used the comb and scissors, no electric clippers.

So finally I got my hair cut. When he had finished cutting, he put me on a chair where all the men were sitting waiting for their hair to be cut. The room was full of cigarette smoke, it was like sitting in a fog, my eyes were smarting and it made me cough. They were talking about football, I remember there were three men cutting hair, those same men were there for years. It was a dark mysterious sort of room, well to a youngster anyway, dark oak panels everywhere, the ladies was on the left as you walked in, a narrow passage to the men's at the back. Mom walked in, looked at me and said, "That's a nice hair cut, you do look smart, has he been OK, Mr Tranter?" "Yes, Mrs, he was fine." She paid him, I think it was 6d (six pence 6). "Bye David," he said as he patted me on the back of my head very hard, "Come again," he said. My mom never knew till years later what that poor barber went through!

SATURDAY MATINEE

The first Saturday matinee I ever went to was at the Atlas Cinema in Stechford, Birmingham, it was just down the road from my house. I went with my sister Doreen, my mom gave her strict instructions not to take me to the back of the cinema where the tip was and not to go through the park after the films had finished.

It was like a stampede to get out, I had never seen so many screaming kids. Doreen took me over the tip, the one Mom said not to (as I got much older I spent many hours on that tip), my sister said, "Don't tell Mom we came the park way home."

As we walked over the tip we came across a big hole at the edge of the tip with a corrugated sheet of metal across one corner of it, someone had been making a den. "I'm going inside," Doreen said, "you stand there and don't stand on this tin it's not safe." As she went in I looked at the tin sheet – it's OK, I won't fall if I stand on it, I thought, so I stood on it; it swivelled because it was resting on two opposite corners. I fell into the hole catching my inside left knee on the corner of the tin sheet, it sliced though my leg like butter, the blood was cascading down my leg, the cut was an inch wide and four inches long.

Thinking a lump of flesh had come out, me and Doreen were searching for the lump of flesh, we thought if we put the flesh back in the hole it would heal up and be OK. "It's gone, Dave," she said, "come on I'll take you to the park keeper." She wrapped her handkerchief round my leg, the blood still cascading down my leg. When the parkie (that's what everyone called him) saw my leg he went white. He wrapped it up with loads of bandages, but the blood came through as soon as he put it on, "You must take him straight to the hospital, that's a very bad cut," he said.

Doreen was crying and by this time I was very pale, losing my strength to walk and feeling very poorly. Poor Mother had a shock, I can't remember any more, whether it's because I passed out from loss of blood I'm not sure. I had eleven stitches and the scar is still very visible to this day. I've never known to this day if Doreen got a good hiding or not, we have never mentioned it since.

ACCIDENT PRONE

Every summer holiday when I was off school for six weeks my mom, bless her, would pray and ask the Lord, "Please don't let David hurt himself this holiday." I was accident prone, it started when I was four years old just before I started school. In our back garden we had a lean-to shed with a flat roof; we climbed on the shed and jumped off – me, my two sisters and my then new-found friend Trevor. This was 1947, it had been raining the ground was very muddy, I was too scared to jump so my sister Janet told me many years later she had pushed me. When I hit the ground I did the splits; I heard a crack – the pain was bad, I lay in the mud screaming. My mom was up the road shopping and my sister Kathleen carried me in to the house. A neighbour came in to the house to see if she could help, "Where does it hurt?" she asked me. I'm lying on the settee in agony and she asked where does it hurt. By this time the house was full of people, a lady kept touching my leg asking, "Does it hurt there?" I said, yes, yes every time she touched me. I heard her say to a woman next to her, "He is stupid, he is saying it hurts no matter where I touch him," (it did). My mom came rushing in, "Oh my baby, what have you done, son?" she was hurting more than I was, "I must take him to the hospital." Mom had no money for the bus fare; she tried to borrow the money for the bus, but no one had any money. When my cousin Arthur who lived with us at that time came home from work he said, "I'll take him on the bus and give my name and address," (that was the done thing then when people had no money). "OK, you do that, and I'll meet you there as soon as I can," said Mom.

After Mom found someone to look after my sisters, with my leg bent in a permanent position my cousin took me to town waited a while, then got back on the bus, got back off the bus at Alum Rock and sat on the wall outside a factory called Southhalls. Why he did what he did I have never known (he could have taken me to any hospital). As he sat on the wall my mom passed on the bus full of panic, she got off at the next stop. My cousin never saw Mom, he got on the bus and took me back home. When Mom got to Southhalls only to find he had gone she too headed back home crying, she flopped in to the chair saying, “Why did you bring him back home?” My cousin replied, “I didn’t know what to do,” (he wasn’t very bright – I was told all this by my mom). “I will take him myself tomorrow.”

So I was in agony all night. Still with my leg bent next day at the hospital the doctor asked, “When did he break his leg, Mother?” “This morning, Doctor,” she replied. “I don’t think so, Mother, it’s started to set – I think he did this last night. Wait outside, Mother,” he told her. With a smile he put his right hand on my heel at the back of my foot, his left hand on the front of my knee, pushed down with his left hand and up with his right – did I scream! Mom came running in, “My baby – what are you doing to him?” “It’s all right, Mother, I’ve only straightened his leg,” he said as though it was nothing, “Now we can X-ray it; he is a big strong boy, Mother.” That didn't help the pain, it turned out I had dislocated my ankle and my knee cap and broken the long bone up the front of my leg from the foot to the knee cap. My leg was plastered and I was given a pair of crutches and taken home in an ambulance – I loved that ambulance ride!

At the age of four if you don't do as you are told by your mother, this is what can happen to you. I never did as I was told – look what happened to me!

HANDFUL OF PENNIES

I loved going to the fair, it was always and still is in the same place; we always called it the Bulls Head Fair, Stechford. The Bulls Head was a pub, I say was because it has now been demolished like so many other pubs in the area.

I'd only had my broken leg out of plaster for a week and I was going to the fair with Trevor and Tony (Trevor's brother). We got off the bus the stop after the Atlas Cinema. It was evening time, the road was quite busy I suppose, Tony and Trevor ran across the road. I looked across and Tony shouted, "Stay there," but I thought the road was clear and I ran across gripping my 11d (eleven pennies) in my hand. A car hit me, I went up in the air doing a somersault and landed on my back, the car had hit my left leg (the one I'd had in plaster), how it never broke again I will never know. The man was shaking, "Get in the car," he didn't know what he was saying, then he said, "Get out of the car," so out I got.

A lady came up to me and said, "Here you are, son, I've picked your pennies up for you, your 9d." "There was 11d," I said. "That's all I found," she answered. There were crowds watching me – I was famous for ten minutes. I limped off to the fair to spend my 9d and the man drove off, I bet it took him a long time to get over that accident, poor man. After a few minutes at the fairground I soon forgot all about it. I'm lucky to be alive.

MY ROCKING HORSE

On my fourth birthday I was given a rocking horse, I remember being so excited, I also remember my sisters were playing on it and they wouldn't get off and let me on it. I stood there crying my little heart out, Mom came into the living room from the kitchen and told them to get off it so on I got and was very happy. My sister Janet was on the back, Doreen on the front, we were having a great time, I will never know how that rocking horse stood up to the treatment we gave it, we treated it very rough. It was a toy and I enjoyed it for many years. I was Hopalong Cassidy one day, Roy Rogers the next, Tex Ritter another, my imagination ran wild. There was one draw back to that rocking horse – if I tried rocking too fast the back legs came up, locked, and threw me over its head.

My mom kept that horse in the coal house; the coal house had a brick-built shelf with concrete slabs on the top which was covering the water pipes, my rocking horse went on there. It just fitted, trouble was it got black from the coal dust, when we had coal that is. If I came off that horse because I rocked too fast Mom would say, "I told you didn't I, if you came off it I would put it back in the coal house, you little bugga," she always called me that, "you will break your neck one of these days," she would say. Every few days I would ask if I could have my horse out to play with, a lot of times she said, "no," because it needed cleaning and she was busy getting the dinners ready for my sisters to have when they came out of school at dinner time. When I did get to play on it Mom would once again say, "if you come off it, back in the coal house." I came off it and back it went. I usually got a nice big lump on my forehead from hitting the floor or the wall. OK, I would think, I will ride my pretend horse, and much to the annoyance of my mother I would hold out my left arm as though I was holding the horse's reins and slapping my backside with my right hand, I would gallop all round the house – I was the sheriff, a cowboy, an Indian, an outlaw, all rolled into one. I think Mom sometimes wished she had let me play in the living room with my rocking horse.

My dad made the horse, he got all the wood from his works. He worked at the Metropolitan Camel Carriage Works, Saltley, Birmingham, where he was a Radial Driller. How Dad got out the wood I have no idea, it was all cut to shape when he brought it out; it was well-seasoned timber and was the same timber they used when building the railway carriages, that's what Dad's firm made – everything to do with railways. My mom's brother Bob, my uncle of course, was a manager at the same works; whether he helped my dad get the timber out I don't know. The metal rockers or stays as my Dad called them were made from 5/16 of an inch round steel which were also bent to shape. Dad did tell me he had a few goes before he got it right, Dad made four other horses for our neighbours, this was ideal for him as my birthday was in October, and the neighbours had seen my horse and asked him to make one for each of their children, and he had time to make all the horses for Christmas. He got everything he needed from work to complete all the horses, even the paint, but he made the mistake of getting paint that needed a coat of special varnish to make it dry, but he didn't know this at the time. After Christmas one of the fathers complained saying their daughter on Christmas morning got paint all over her and ruined her new clothes, my horse was OK, he must have used different paint for mine. Janet my sister had my rocking horse for twenty years, my brother John took a pattern off it and made some horses, he gave me one so I took it to Janet's and swopped it for my horse – it sits in the corner of my bedroom now, and every time I look at it the memories of my childhood are fondly remembered. You can see from the pictures how the legs locked and threw me over its head.

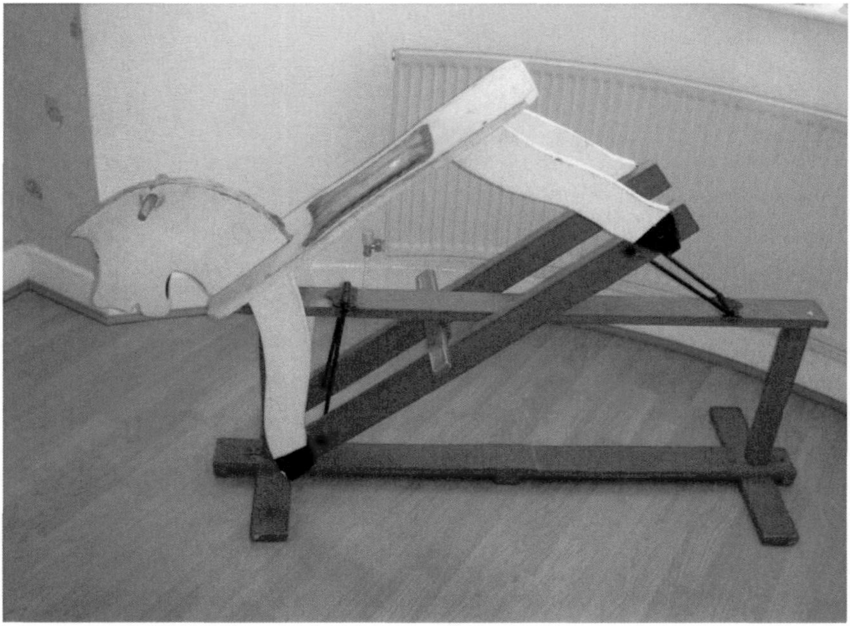

My rocking horse – showing the locked back legs.

Every time I played on my rocking horse I would go too fast and was thrown over its head. I always got told off by my mom, and the horse was put back in the coal house.

LEFTOVERS

I have heard people say when they were children all the food their parents had always seemed better than what they had. I was just the same when my dad came home from work which was usually late because he always dropped in to the Tote, which was a club by his works. Dropped in means he was drinking. When he sat down to dinner I used to stand and watch him eating, this used to annoy him, “What do you want?” he would say in a stern voice. “Can I have some meat please?” he handed me his fork with the meat on it and said, “Gad Blimey,” that was his favourite saying and the other two words that went with that I just cannot repeat, or do not wish to, it was his way of saying, I am annoyed. He would cut a piece of meat and hand it to me, attached to it was his fork, it always tasted much better to me than mine just because it was Dad’s. I would stand there chewing and he would order me to go and play, so I always went into the kitchen waited a couple of minutes and strolled back into the living room and sat on the settee, this was facing forward to where the dining table was. I just kept a low profile, thinking he wouldn’t notice. When he had finished eating he would always push his plate away from him and wipe his fingers on the tablecloth. Quick as a flash I would jump up and look on Dad’s plate to see if anything was left; if there was, I would say, “Please can I have that, Dad?” I had to be quick for fear someone else in the room would get there before me, “Go on,” he would say as he rose from the dining room chair to the easy chair by the fire. No matter what was left I ate it – greedy no, hungry yes I was.

As soon as Dad sat in his easy chair by the fire he lit up his Woodbine cigarette, and as it got dark the flickering flames from the fire danced all over the ceiling, that holds such special memories. Cosy and feeling very secure. I would play ‘I Spy’ with my sisters, we only had a wireless, we didn’t have a television for several years. Playing ‘I Spy’ was a laugh because I couldn’t read. My sister would say, “I spy with my little eye something beginning with H." I would say, door, window, rug – they were very patient with me.

I also remember a lot of times when the fire was aglow and kept glowing by putting one lump of coal on at a time, it was those times when I went out and pulled the palings off the neighbours' fences for firewood. When we did have five hundred weight of coal delivered, Mom would on a Sunday, "have a nice fire going." When evening came curtains drawn, once again those flickering dancing images on the ceiling, even on the walls, on a cold winter's night would warm me right through. Many times we would all sit in the dark with the fire aglow – Kathleen, Doreen, Janet, John in his pram, Mom and Dad and me. Dad smoking his Woodbine, the rest of us just staring into the fire not a word being said. It's a warm feeling remembering those family evenings.

JACK FROST

Every year when winter came round our house was very cold and damp. Every morning there were beautiful patterns in ice on the inside of our windows, the colours were sparkling when the sun shone on them, the ice was so thick when I tried to scratch it with my nail nothing happened. We had lino on the floor and when I got out of bed half asleep and put my foot on the floor I soon woke up, it was like standing on ice. I only possessed one shirt, I hadn't any pyjamas so I slept in my shirt. I slept with my younger brother, he wet the bed every night, so every morning I was soaking wet.

My mom lit the oven so we could stand in front of it, steam rising off us. I had to go to school every day with that same shirt on. I tucked my collar inside so I could wash my neck. One shirt, a pair of pumps with holes in, socks and a coat I could not fasten because it was too small – that was my entire wardrobe. We only possessed one towel, being the two youngest when we came to use the towel it was soaking wet. On a very cold snowy and frosty morning feeling very cold and drying oneself on a wet towel was, to say the least, not nice. Mom would say, "You will be all right, dry yourself." I went through that longer than I care to remember. We had a blue long family comb, which sat on the window sill next to the back door; again we only had one and it was used by the whole family. We had that comb for years.

I got two slices of toast most mornings, on rare occasions we got porridge. I always, all through my school years, took two pieces of toast for my lunch wrapped in some of the bread paper; I put them in my coat pocket and by break time they were all screwed up like someone had twisted them round.

Years earlier I slept in a bed with my two sisters, they were at the top of the bed, I was at the bottom; yes we had arguments about feet every night, most times I did it on purpose. In the winter Mom put a house brick in the oven, wrapped it up and put it in the bed, even a pop bottle filled with warm water was used when we had one. On occasions the water would leak out of the bottle and wet the bed because we hadn't screwed the stopper up tight enough, which wasn't often because there was a deposit on pop bottles then. I've taken them back to get the deposit for my mom then bought two pounds of spuds with the 3d (three pence) I got off the bottle, it could have been 2d I got in those early days. When my eldest brother came home on leave from the army his overcoat was put on our bed, it felt very heavy and very warm. I was told many times by my mom, "There are people out there worse off than you, are," all I can say to that is they must have been naked and lived under a tree.

Our toilet, being outside, froze up every winter. My mom took a bucket to bed; we all would go into her bedroom to use it, we shivered all the way there and back. My mom worked so hard for her children as most mothers do, she was always first up and suffered those cold 'jack frost bitten' mornings to warm the kitchen up for all her family and do the breakfast for us and Dad's lunch for work. As we all left school and joined the ranks of workers Mom still did the same every morning but now she had lunches to do as well. How these mothers cope, I have no idea, but they do – my hat goes off to those brave ladies, all of them.

IN ALL ITS GLORY

Barry's parents who lived next door sometimes took me with them when they had a picnic and the males, including Barry, would be fishing. This trip was a short time after I fell in the river at Colsehill when I went with Barry, and his dad took us home in his Scammel Scarab – that being his three-wheeled Railway Iron Horse.

We got on the 14 bus at Glebe Farm, where we went I've no idea, wherever it was, we were there all day, while they were fishing. I wondered off, I don't like fishing, I got bored – well young children do don't they. There was a barbed wire fence – what's in there, I thought, so under I go, caught my trousers on the barbed wire and heard the sound of ripping material. Well it had torn my trousers, how can I say, like an upside down U, it made a flap. I had no underpants on, (the reason being that I didn't possess any), so I tucked it in the best I could, made sure no one could see, and sat on the grass by the men fishing. When all was packed up off we went, me walking at the side of them holding my trousers where they were ripped, on the bus liking the bus ride got off the bus and completely forgot about my trousers. I was walking in front of them with Barry, they were all laughing, I looked round to see why they were laughing. Barry's mom, holding her stomach while in fits of laughter, said in muffled voice through the laughter, "What have you done to your trousers?" By this time they were all in fits of laughter – Barry's two sisters, his older brother and mom and dad. Of course I was showing both cheeks of my bare bum, it must have looked a sight, and my face felt red.

On arriving home my mom was not too pleased as she had to find something to patch these trousers for me to wear them to go to school in. The patch was red on my grey trousers, she had tried very hard to find some material that was suitable, she even asked her friend Lizzie but she didn't have anything and the trousers had to be patched as they were the only ones I possessed so she had no choice but to patch them as I needed them for school. Even though we lived in poverty I had a wonderful childhood and my mother always did the best she could.

SUFFERING

I remember one very cold winter's evening in 1949 to 1950; the fire in the grate was only just glowing, five of us we were very cold, Mom was rubbing our hands and giving us a cuddle to warm us up, Dad nowhere to be seen, seeing my mom cry because her little children were cold and hungry.

That evening started me on the road to pulling off the palings in my garden and down my road. It was snowing and without gloves my hands soon got cold, no overcoat, no wellingtons, only pumps with holes in. The fence then was low, it was feather-edge fencing about two and a half feet high. All the front gardens at that time had the same fencing, it was put there by the council. I was able to pull off the palings which were about four inches wide; some came away with no trouble, others I used one of the palings to put behind them and prise them off. With an armful I took them home thinking Mom would be pleased, but I got a severe telling off and told, "Never take what isn't yours." I cried like a baby, she kissed and hugged me. After that I used to break them up and put them in the coal house; we had no coal so I knew Mom wouldn't go in there. I became quite good at getting those palings off. At the end of that winter the palings in my road had a lot of gaps. Mom asked me to go to the tip to find some old shoes so she could burn them on the fire – with slack and potato peelings they made a good fire. I found many shoes on that tip, I even went there with my friend Trevor. I made a trolley and a bike off that tip but that's another story.

I can say though, I loved my childhood, the freedom to roam to explore – I am very grateful for that.

LAUGHTER

When my mom used to tell me my eldest brother Donald was coming home on leave from the army, I used to shake with fear. I think he loved to hear screams with pain attached to them. Mom would say, "Oh that's good," as she read his letter, "he's coming home for the weekend." "Oh no," I used to say to myself. I used to hide and stay out of his way.

When I was out playing I completely forgot about Donald coming home from the army. In I went to have my tea through the back kitchen and into the living room. Then absolute and total fear stormed through my little body. Sitting on the chair by the living room door was Donald. "Got you!" he would say as he grabbed my arm. "You forgot about me didn't you," he would say. "Have you been playing up?" he would ask. "No," I would say. He would turn me over his knee and bite my bum. I'm not going to cry, I used to think to myself, but the pain was unbearable. I held back the tears and Donald would say, "Oh tough are we now!" Over his knee again, and boy did he bite. "YES!" I screamed very loud and cried for a long time. I had big teeth marks and very bad bruising, it was tender and very sore for a long time. He laughed very loud and thought it was funny. I didn't think it was funny. It turned out he had been told not to hit the kids. He would say, "Well I haven't hit him, I only bit his bum."

My two eldest brothers were throwing my sister Janet up to the ceiling and catching her as she was coming down; she was laughing and having a good time, enjoying every moment of it, I was saying, "My turn, do it to me, do it to me," so they threw me up in the air turned and walked away. I hit the floor, crying. They seemed to think this was very funny as the two of them were laughing. Mom said, "Why don't you leave him alone and Donald replied, "We're only playing, he's alright." It seemed they thought what they did to me didn't matter.

MAGGOTY BROOK

At the age of five my sister Doreen (aged eight) took me and my sister Janet (aged six) over the park to what was called the white bridge, which was so called because it was painted white. This was in the Bucklands End area, the road name is Colehall Lane. At that time in 1948 all the new houses were being built, we explored the unfinished houses without doors so it wasn't a problem getting in, it was fun to me. I had never seen houses being built, I was really fascinated. Just by the end house we had been looking at was the River Cole, the white bridge spanned it of course, and about eight yards from the bridge was what I was told was a spring with its fresh water, known as Maggoty Brook. Everyone, all the children, called it that, but I've no idea why or who gave it that name. We all drank from this clear water spring, myself on many occasions as I was growing up. This spring ran into the River Cole.

All those houses I saw being built at the age of five have, in the last couple of years, been demolished and now new houses stand where they were; such a short time for houses to stand 1948–2008. I wonder if Maggoty Brook is still there? I must go and look and relive my memory of a five-year-old. I may see you there. By the way, the white bridge is no longer there. One year we had very bad storms, the swollen river broke its banks, lifted that old white bridge and floated it down the river. A temporary bridge was erected, single line traffic only, traffic lights each end of it. I was told it was temporary, but it is still there years later. I wonder how much longer it will be there across the river, will it outlive the new houses? At least it slows the traffic down which is a good thing, especially at night as it is very dark in that area.

My sister had a den under all the overhanging trees, brambles and shrubs, it was great, I really loved it. I went there a few times with a friend of mine; to think then I was six years old, being allowed to go all over the place. All Mom used to say and she said it all the time was, "Mind the horse road," and those sayings never changed. I bet those sayings are still said today by some of the older generation to young children. Mom would say things like, "Where have you been?" the answer was always, "Nowhere." Mom would usually ask, "What you been doing?" our reply was always, "Nothing." "I don't know, you have been out all day, been nowhere and done nothing," she always replied. Been down the park to me was going nowhere, playing, was doing nothing, not like running errands or going up to town.

So many things we do as children that as adults gives us such wonderful memories to look back on, especially in an evening sitting alone in a darkened room with just the reflection of the fire flickering and dancing round the room, just like the evenings when we sat with our mother. What wonderful feelings run through my mind when remembering those halcyon days.

FAMILY PUDDINGS

Mom was a wonderful cook, self-taught on most recipes, but my nan of course showed her how to do many dishes. Her bread pudding was so tasty, I used to help her to mix it up, I loved the feel of that mixture on my hands. Fruit cake we sometimes had, I was never allowed to touch that. My brothers and sisters used to stand around the kitchen table and we would fight to see who could get the bowl and scrape out the mixture that was left. If you were lucky enough to be there on your own Mom used to let me scrape out the bowl to myself.

The food I didn't like eating was tripe, chitterlings, brains and kidneys. Even if I was hungry I couldn't eat those items of food. Apple pies was my favourite. It was fascinating to watch Mom doing the pastry. She used to use a sterilised milk bottle as a rolling pin, sprinkling flour everywhere – it used to be all over the floor and all over Mom's pinny – I can see her doing that now. I would help to peel the apples, I used to eat all the apple peel, the core, pips as well. After all the pastry that was left after doing the apple pie, Mom used to allow one of us that was there at the time to make jam cakes with it. She always put a pattern around the pies and a pattern in the middle. Also a slit in the middle to let the steam come out. I used to feel very clever when I made the jam cakes with the leftover pastry and say to my sister, "I've made this." My mom used to always make me share it. When she made mince pies, after rolling out the pastry, she would get a set of metal cutters that she bought from Woolworths for 6d (sixpence). These were used mostly at Christmas for mince pies. She always allowed her children to use the cutters to cut the shapes out of the pastry, and it was very exciting to me to see the shapes they made.

Another pudding I used to love was suet pudding, known as Spotted Dick. After mixing the mixture Mom would always place it into a pillow case or a tea towel and put it into a pan of water to boil. One pudding I hated was Yorkshire Pudding with jam on it. I used to eat it but never liked it. I was never keen on rice pudding but I loved semolina and still do.

One food item that I did like that Mom made was brawn. Mom used to buy pigs' heads from the butcher's, scrub them clean, put her fingers in the eyeball sockets and pull out the eyes. The head was then boiled in a pan and that was one smell I hated. The brawn, when it was done and set, was even better than when it was brought from the butchers. Cooking is one thing that I have never taken to, I used to watch my mom do all the baking. All the ingredients were never measured, she just guessed them. She was so good she got the weight close enough to the nearest ounce.

If we knew Mom was going to bake the next day my sister Janet and Trevor's sister Nanette, Trevor and myself would go scrumping apples when it was dark.

The one time I remember as we crept out of one of the gardens, my sister Janet had filled her knickers with apples and Nanette, to our amazement, was dragging behind her a branch full of apples. When we asked her why she had broken off a branch she replied, "I couldn't be bothered picking the apples and filling my knickers with them so I broke off this branch." We were all surprised at the amount of apples that were on the branch, we ate some of the apples and we took the rest to our moms, our moms always told us off but seeing that we couldn't take them back Mom made a beautiful apple pie. Of course it always depended on whether Mom had enough flour, lard, eggs and whatever else one needs to make pies with – usually we got our pie.

It must be the end of the season

"OK, Trev, that's enough. I hope they are sweet. I'll take some home to my mom – she might make an apple pie."
"Yeah, me too, Dave. I'll take some to my mom as well."

A PERFECT RIGHT HAND

In 1949 I had been in school for about seven months; I started in the January of that year, a tender five-year-old. I was asked with all the other boys and girls to take home a letter telling parents about a day out at Whipsnade Zoo, and would they sign the consent form to allow their sons or daughters to go on the coach and would they pay 3d (three pence) a week or more as the cost of the trip was 10/- (ten shillings). I don't recall paying the 3d every week, I do however remember saying to my teacher on one occasion that I hadn't any money to give to her and she shouted at me in a very loud voice and shamed me in front of the whole class, by saying that all the other boys and girls had paid, so why couldn't I? What did they expect a five-year-old to do at that time when children relied on their parents, it was all my mom could do to feed us.

Anyway I did go on the trip, my teacher and the headmistress came with us. I can still see that screwed-up face of that headmistress – I hated her, talk about ruling a child with a rod of iron, that headmistress had two iron rods and a whip, her voice was the whip, her hands were the rods of iron, her right-hand slap could make you have nightmares for a fortnight. I remember nothing of the day at Whipsnade Zoo, only that one incident that is burned in my memory. Can't remember that head teacher's name nor do I want to.

There was a fairground ride which had a barrier all round it so no one could walk into the ride and get hurt; being five years old and very small I put my hands on top of the rail and ducked my head under it. I was about six feet away from the ride going up and down and round and round. I remember the horses on the ride because I was wishing I could sit on one and have a ride, when I was suddenly violently dragged away by my hair, screamed at and slapped around the face from left to right until I felt sick and giddy.

That's what I remember about that day at Whipsnade Zoo. I've tried but I remember nothing, only that part of the day. I had only been there ten minutes when that happened. I do remember wanting to go home to someone that loved me, my mom.

DINNERS – ONE DAY ONLY

My first week at school I heard the children saying how much they enjoyed the dinners and puddings they had had that day, the thought of puddings made me want school dinners. The boy who became my friend stayed for school dinners and told me all about them. His name was Michael Luckman, we were never apart, he never once made any comment on my appearance, sadly he died of Leukaemia at the tender age of 14. I think of him even to this day. We were in the junior football team, we won the league in 1955; he is standing next to me on my left, right as you look at the photograph (see on page 204–5 back row far right).

My mom had to plead and beg the headmistress to let me stay for school dinners (Mom told me that) because Mom didn't work so I wasn't really allowed. Only certain children got free meals; my mom paid for that week. I heard girls taking the mick out of the children who had free dinners, saying, "Our moms have to pay so why should you get them free, your parents are scroungers."

So for my first school dinner, I was a little excited, we had to line up in the corridor to go into the hall where all the table and chairs were placed out in two rows. As I stood in the queue the girls were saying to me, "You can't stand by me," so I ended up at the back of the queue. In we went in single file; every time I went to sit down I was told, "You can't sit by me." The teacher must have seen what was going on, she told me to sit there, pointing to a vacant chair, and I sat opposite the cruellest girl I have ever known who said, "Why did she put you opposite me?" She made me feel terrible, "You sit somewhere else tomorrow, I don't want you looking at me." We had fish for dinner; on the table was a bottle of parsley sauce, I never knew what it was then, so I picked it up and shook it hard – it smothered my dinner, I was horrified! The girl started at me again, "I bet you never have sauce in your house, bet your parents can't afford it, you only put that much sauce on because you are a pig!" I tried to eat it but found I didn't like it, so I didn't have any dinner. We had apple pie and custard for desert and the girl opposite said, "I see you have eaten all that, I bet you never get deserts at home."

The reason I shook the parsley sauce bottle the way I did was because at home we always had to shake the brown sauce like that. I only said half a dozen words all through dinner. The last words I remember her saying to me were, "Anyway you shouldn't be here!" She was so cruel I had tears in my eyes.

When I went home that evening from school I told my mom I wasn't staying for school dinners anymore. My mom went mad at me, saying, "After all the pleading and begging I did to your headmistress and now you don't want to stay for dinners any more and I paid for the whole week." "I don't like the school dinners," I said. I never told her the real truth. The truth was I was to afraid to sit opposite that cruel girl and be tormented. That was my first and last school dinner. That girl was right about the pudding, we rarely got them at home. I wonder what she is like now? I bet she doesn't remember what a horrible cruel girl she was.

AN APPLE A DAY

When I started school, the second teacher I had was called Miss Pitt, I loved that teacher. One day while she was telling us something she suddenly said, “David, come here.” I remember this moment so well. When I got to her desk she opened the drawer, took out an apple, she held it out to me and said, “Here is an apple for you,” placed it in my hand and started to say, “but,” but the apple went straight to my mouth that fast I think she was going to say, “don’t eat it until playtime.”

What a wonderful lady. With me standing there, devouring the apple, she said, “Alright, David, go and sit down and eat it as quietly as you can.” I was so thin and so poorly dressed, I think maybe I was malnourished and she could see that. Every day that very thoughtful wonderful lady brought me an apple. After that first day she gave me an apple she would say, “I’m going to give you an apple at playtime,” which she did. I do so love that lady, thank you Miss Pitt and God bless her.

My teacher, Miss Pitt, giving me an apple

MY FIRST TRAM RIDE

It's funny the things that trigger your memory. My first tram ride was to the Lickey Hills, this I remember very well after my wife jogged my memory. I was five years old, before my younger brother John was born. Mom took me and my three sisters Janet, Doreen and Kathleen to the Lickey Hills on a tram. We travelled on a number 14 bus from Audley Road, Glebe Farm, Stechford Birmingham 33, into Birmingham city centre. I can remember getting off the bus in the Old Square, from here we walked through the Minories which fascinated me because the road had been laid with rubber blocks. We walked under Lewis's bridge across Bull Street along Temple Row until we reached St. Phillips church (this was the church I attended for my school leavers' service at the age of fifteen), we crossed over the church yard leading us to Colmore Row, walked along this busy road to the end. Across the road on the left-hand side stood the Post Office with what to me seemed a very large revolving door; on the left of this building was Hill Street, which was quite a steep hill going down, crossing over the railway bridge the walls of which were much too high to see over but at least I could smell and hear the trains. At the bottom of this hill we turned into Navigation Street and to my amazement a wonderful sight to see all the trams lined up with queues of people waiting to get on, what seemed to me at that time hundreds of people.

Once I was on the tram, I was so excited; even at the tender age of five I loved trains, the clickety-clack sound they made on the rails. I had never been on a train at that time. Me and my new friend Trevor went to Stechford railway station to watch the trains go by, we were allowed to roam all over the place and at such a young age, so going on a tram seemed to me like going on a train. The swaying and the clickety-clack was just a dream to me, I can still see those polished wooden benches with the reversible back rests. I was sitting by the window looking at the world going by, I was so happy, what I thought I was doing was whistling. My sister

Kathleen who was sitting on the other side of the tram opposite me shouted to me, "David, for God's sake shut up." Mom said to her, "Oh leave him alone, he's just happy," so I stopped whistling, I bet to the delight of the passengers!

When we arrived at the terminus this was situated at the bottom of the Lickey Hills, well almost. I remember what seemed to me like a thousand steps to go up, and I ran up those steps in my excitement to see what was at the top, it was all trees all around. Mom being a large lady struggled to climb those steps (I bet they are still there). Mom took sandwiches and a bottle of pop. I thought I would roll down the hill and I went much faster than I thought I would – it made me very giddy, and as I stood up I fell over, my sense of balance was all over the place. As I finally regained my senses I went exploring; I remember thinking, I'm going to be an explorer, as boys do. I strayed further away from my mom than I should have, when I suddenly realised I was lost. I was quietly starting to panic – how long I was away from my family I'm not sure. I wondered around aimlessly looking for them, then to my delight I saw them through the bushes sitting on a bench eating sandwiches and drinking pop. I waited a couple of minutes to calm myself down then I slowly walked up to them and said, "I've been exploring – can I have a sandwich please, I'm hungry." "I'll give you sandwich, my lad, I've been worried to death," Mom said sternly. "Why?" I asked calmly, trying to act like I didn't know. "Right, you stay where I can see you." "OK, Mom," I replied, no way was I going to explore anymore, I was afraid of getting lost again, so I played with my sisters until Mom shouted, "Come on, you lot, we are going back now." Yeah, I thought, back on that tram.

I was overjoyed. To me that was the best part of the day out, riding on that tram, it's a shame that young people can't experience riding round the cities on a tram the same as the ones I rode on.

IRON HORSE

My next-door neighbours' son was named Barry, he was five years older than me. He loved the small hours of the morning, and boy could he talk, he could talk the leg off an iron pot as the saying goes. No matter how tired I became he just would not go home. I made friends with Barry as soon as I started to walk, we sort of hit it off from day one, we played together and kept in touch until the day he died, which was in the year 2009 – a sad loss of a very dear friend.

Looking back to his and my childhood, when I was only six years old he took me to a place called Coleshill. He loved fishing, and the thing I remember about that day and the reason I remember it was that there were stepping stones going across the river, one was very green with moss. The river was quite shallow where the stepping stones were, I remember like it was yesterday, his very words to me, "Mind how you step on this stone it's very slippy." Not taking a lot of notice and thinking I knew best I jumped on to that stone, yes jumped! Of course, I slipped and fell in, Barry looked at me and laughed, he said, "I told you it was slippy." To a skinny six-year-old the water seemed to be deep, it came past my waist, Barry wadded in, picked me up and carried me to the bank. (That wasn't the last time I went into the river while I was growing up, it happened a few times; that first soaking I got was at the bottom of a hill in Coleshill called Maxstoke Lane, the river is the Blythe. I spent many a happy hour over the following years in that same field, the difference was that I had swimming trunks.)

As we started to walk across the field to head home Barry saw an LMS railway three-wheeler lorry, he ran very quickly to the gate and waved like mad with his coat – talk about luck or coincidence, it turned out it was Barry's dad (he had worked on the railways from a boy, his depot was in Nechells in Rupert Street, Birmingham). Barry shouted, "Come on, Dave, it's my dad." Barry's dad looked at me and smiled, he never laughed, he could see I was distressed because I was soaking wet, "And what happened to you, young man?" he asked as if he didn't know. "I fell into the river," I replied. "Come on, young fella," he said, "I will take you home in my Iron Horse." "Iron Horse?" I said. "Yes, David, that's what they call these lorries, Iron Horses – look," he said, "you sit on the cowling, you'll get dry on there."

I got lovely and warm sitting on that cowling, it was a cover that fitted over the engine, I loved that lorry, I thought to myself I'm going to drive one of these when I grow up. When I did grow up I passed my test on those Iron Horses, I really loved driving them and would you believe it I worked alongside Barry's Dad! When I called him by his surname, which I had done from birth, he said, "David, you're an adult now – call me Bunny." Calling him by his first name was very strange to me because I was brought up to say Mr and Mrs and if I didn't my mom would clout me round the ear so it was always by their surname which I still do to this day.

Incidentally, the correct name for the three-wheel Iron Horse is Scammel Scarab.

TWO BIRTHDAY CARDS

I've sat and thought very hard about this. Did I ever get a present for my birthday? I cannot bring to mind any. I did get a windjammer as they were called at that time, just before my ninth birthday – I felt really smart and very warm, well I could fasten it up. I suppose that could be classed as a present, well it was a wonderful gift, I loved it, being brown in colour and zipped right up to the neck.

Trevor was so jealous, on that same morning I was showing it to Trevor I didn't see him pick up a handful of dirt, and as we were talking he threw the dirt over my new coat and ran off like the wind into his house. I ran after him, knocked on his back door, his mom came and said, "Trevor told me to tell you he doesn't feel well, he is not playing out today." We laughed about it the next day, we never fell out so I did it to him the first chance I had, which was a long time after my brother got married in the December. I wore that coat for his wedding – maybe that's why I got the new coat, but I wasn't allowed to play out in it till after the wedding.

One year I remember well, I was nine years old, Trevor's Mom, my mom's best friend Lizzie, gave me a birthday card every year; this year was different, I got a postcard birthday card, that's the type we used to get. The year I was nine she put 2/- (two shillings) in with the card, the first and last time that happened. Some years I got two cards – one off my mom and one off Trevor's mom. I never, as far as I know, got a present, it just never happened, Most years I only got one card. Well, better I ate food than had a toy car or a game.

MY FIRST CAR RIDE

My first car accident was in the year 1950, when cars owned by the working classes were few and far between. How it came about was my two eldest brothers were converting a fish and chip van into a caravanette; the chip van was equipped with all its fryers still in situ and all the fat still in it, it was smelling of old grease and chip fat everywhere, horrible. I don't think buying your fish and chips from this van would have been a good idea. Any road up, I was given a scraper to get as much fat as I could off the walls – "Don't get dirty" was my eldest brother's command. I ask you, fat and grease everywhere. I obeyed his every wish, well I tried to, yes I got grease and fat on me. "Leave that now," he said, "it's OK," so very quickly I dropped the scraper. I stood and watched him sawing slots in a piece of 2x2 inch timber – I want to do that, I thought, and picked up a saw and started to saw one of the slots he had been sawing. I will soon get through this, I thought, he will be pleased with me (secretly I thought he would give me some money for helping him – WRONG). Suddenly a deafening shout of, "Don't cut through that, put the saw down," my nerves took on an Olympic high jump. What he explained when he came back down to earth was when a piece has many slots cut in it you can bend it, pointing to the round front of an old caravan, "that's what these two pieces of wood will do, form a round front over the driver's cab." All this took place on an old farm, not long before it was demolished. The changing face of old England, you would never know there had been a farm there. It looked far better than it does now, it was only a couple of miles from where I lived.

My dad came to see how they were doing with this old van, he was very impressed with them. A few minutes after Dad arrived my eldest brother Donald's friend George turned up (he lived across the road from our house, they grew up together, even evacuated together somewhere, I think it was Nottingham). This friend arrived in a brand new car, he had only had it a week, a bright shiny black car, the smell of the leather interior is something I shall never forget. Sometime later my brother decided to pack up and go home, George said, "Come on, I'll give you a lift in my new car."

I was very excited; a ride in a car, I had never been in a car before! Out of the farm gate, turned right, it felt like we were doing a thousand miles an hour, well it was fast. I remember these words my dad said to me, "Hang on to your hat, son, this is the fastest you will ever go down this road." We were flying, we came to the railway bridge (this bridge has since been widened), and started to climb to reach the brow of the bridge; there wasn't any way of seeing if there were any other vehicles coming over the bridge on the other side. Just as we reached the brow George was too far over to the right. We slammed straight into an oncoming vehicle and it folded up like cardboard. The poor man sat with a glazed look on his face, his car was absolutely smashed up. George had pushed the car right up against the bridge wall so the man could not get out of any of the doors. My dad told me to go home and tell Mom he would be late home for dinner. I ran like the wind non-stop until I reached home, puffing and panting for breath. I blurted out, "We have been in a car smash, Mom, and it's all smashed up!" Poor Mother went white, staggered to her chair, sat down with tears streaming down her face. "Oh my god!" Mom thought the way I told her was that they had all been smashed up and were all in hospital. "Where are they, where are they?" she kept saying. I was confused, I couldn't understand why she was so upset, she stood up and started running round the room like a headless chicken. "Oh," I said calmly, "I forgot to tell you Dad said he would be a little late home for dinner." Once again she staggered to the chair, nerves all shot. With a stare she says to me, "You silly little bugga, I thought your dad and brother had been seriously injured." I replied in a calm voice, "No, the car's been smashed up not the men, there's nothing wrong with them they're OK." I learned in later years from my brother Donald that even though it was George's fault the insurance company would not pay out. Both men blamed each other for the accident. It turned out that the poor man had repaired his engine, he had no tax or insurance and was out testing the engine he had just repaired. What a shame, I thought, that nice shiny car is all scratched. I remember I was not frightened or shaken at all I was very calm. That was my first car accident.

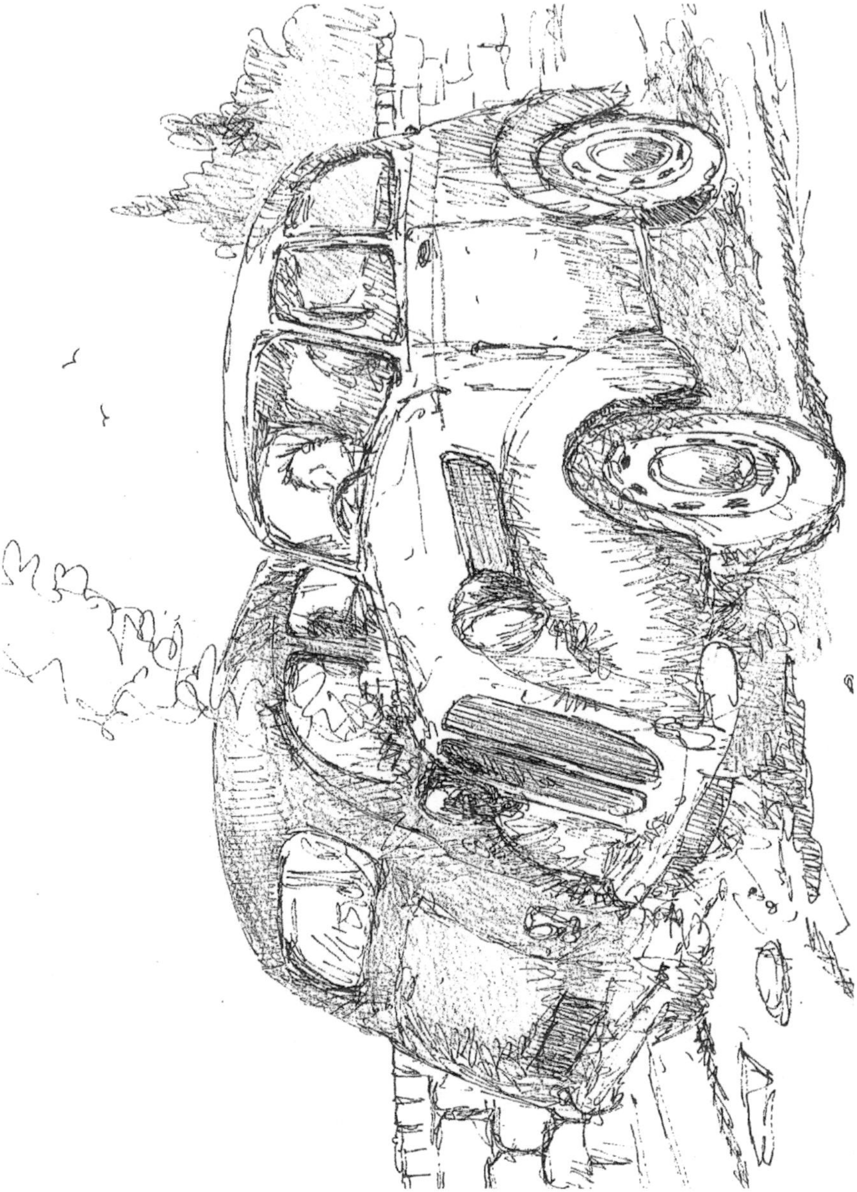

Scraping by

The bridge of my first car accident in Church Road, Stechford

Scene of my first car accident,
showing the bridge from the other side of Church Lane.

STREAMERS

Stanley James was a hardware shop that was in Glebe Farm, Birmingham 33. In the past my mom bought linoleum from there, we always called it lino, it was the cheapest form of floor covering you could get at that time; it looked beautiful when first laid down, bright vibrant colours, but after a very short time if it carried a lot of traffic the pattern soon wore off. My mom always fitted the lino, never my dad.

Mom even did all the painting and decorating, she was brilliant at wallpaper hanging. Back in the 1940s the edge was left on the wallpaper, but for a small fee the paper was put on a machine and it cut nearly through the edging. When the roll was taped on the table the cut edge would fall off. When Mom couldn't afford to pay the extra money to have the rolls trimmed she would sit for what seemed like hours and cut off the edge with a pair of scissors. I have seen Mom leave the edge on, but when put on the wall and overlapped a bulge from top to bottom of the edge could be seen on every strip. It didn't look too bad, I went in many houses and saw paper hung like that, in fact I helped my mom to hang paper like that. When I was about seven or eight, after she had cut off the edge I always asked to have the edges to play with; she always said no but with a lot of nagging she would give in. I was told, "Don't throw them in the horse road, put it in the dustbin when you have finished playing with them," but after me and my friends had thrown them at each other and had lots of fun I got fed up rolling them up so I left them, streamers scattered all over the road. Yes again I was told to get the cane from the coal house, it was too late to say sorry, three whacks across the bum so I ended up picking it all up after all. When Mom folded her arms and said to do it, you did it or get the cane from the coal house. Children never learn do they? Well I never did, that's a fact.

GROWING ANOTHER HEAD

Before I started school I had a bubble grow out of the side of my head, you could see the blood pumping round it. I was taken to the Children's Hospital in Birmingham city. When the doctor looked at it he was puzzled. He didn't know what it was or why it had happened. I heard him say to my mother, "I won't bandage it, let the air get to it, it looks like an artery that has grown out of his head." He took Mother to one side, he must have thought I was deaf, but in a low voice I heard him say, "Whatever happens, Mother, he must not make it bleed, or he could bleed to death." Well I was frightened to death! Those words frightened the life out of me, as a young child they would wouldn't they and did. After that day I did make it bleed many times and every time I would run to my mom saying, "Mom it's bleeding, am I going to die?" at the same time crying my eyes out. I used to turn over in bed and make it bleed and the pillow used to be covered in blood. The worst time it bled (and boy did it bleed) I was friendly fighting with my cousin who lived with us at the time. He was the one that took me on the bus when I broke my leg. He suddenly said to me, "You're bleeding." I went to my mom, screaming and again saying, "Am I going to die, am I am going to die?" She ran the tap, and with my head under the tap she just kept bathing it with a wet rag. The rag got soaked in blood, it was everywhere. My mom was crying while she was doing it. It seemed a long time being done but it did stop eventually. That was the most worrying time of my young life. But it did go away, it just started to go down. I do believe the doctor was putting some sort of ointment on it to slowly freeze it and it disappeared.

When playing with my friends once they were surprised to see blood pumping from it when I headed a ball. Many years later my mom said that she was worried to death and thought she was going to lose me every time it bled. My mother should never have been put through an ordeal such as that because her life was hard enough.

ICED GEMS

My mom was known by all the local shopkeepers because she used those shops all through the war. People got preferential treatment if they used the same shops. I remember my mom going into Wrenson's (they are no longer trading) asking for a quarter of a pound of iced gems, those little biscuits with a dab of icing sugar in the middle of the biscuit. "Sorry, you are not one of my regular customers," said Mr O the manager. I believe these were still on rationing. My mom wasn't very happy to hear him say that to her so she told him a few home truths. Her friend Winnie used Wrenson's all the time and went in and bought iced gems for her. Mr O the manager asked Winnie, "Are you buying these for her?" and she replied, "I'm buying them for myself and it's none of your business what I buy!"

My mom was very hard up and she used to make me go to Holidays the local butcher. She used this butcher all through the war and I used to have to go and ask for two pence worth of bones for the dog (he knew we didn't have a dog). He always went to the back of his shop and gave me lots of bones wrapped in newspaper and he always said, "Tell Dora, I mean your mom, they haven't been on the floor and there is quite a lot of meat still on the bone." Mom made a stew with them and made it last for three or four days – that's living, eh?

PEG RUGS

When Trevor and I were collecting rags to make money, my mom went through the rags to see if there were any coats she could cut up; there were two coats, and I helped my mom to cut them up into long strips about one inch wide by six inches long, so she could make peg rugs. The lengths of material were looped through a piece of canvas, and the different colours of the material were sometimes made into a pattern.

It took me and my mom some time to make a peg rug, but I really enjoyed making them with my mom and my sisters sitting in front of the fire. Mom lined the back with oddments of materials, and when placed in front of the fire it was a joy to sit on.

I had one once at the side of my bed, and I was sitting on it one day when I saw loads of silver things. I asked Mom what they were, she called them silver fish; I used to watch them running around, and if I moved they would vanish very quickly.

I was told sometimes to put the peg rug on the line and beat it with the yard broom; the dust that used to come out of it was all from the fire and ashes, and I ended up all grey from the ash dust.

These rugs looked good when down and lasted a very long time.

BIRMINGHAM POST AND MAIL

The first year of the juniors the teacher called me out; I went to the desk where she was sitting writing a letter which she folded and handed to me, saying, "Take this letter and give it to your mother." "OK, Miss," I said. I went to sit down. "No," she said. "Take it home to your mom now." "What, leave school now Miss?" "Yes go straight home now."

I think it was about 2.30–3.00 p.m. Well, get out of school! My feet went so fast through the playground before she changed her mind. My mom's face when I walked in, "What are you doing out of school?" "My teacher said I could leave school and give you this letter." Well Mom was so delighted when she read the letter she rushed in to the hall for her coat and said, "Come on quick, we can get there in time." We ran up the road and caught the bus. "Where are we going?" I asked. "Shh," she said. I just didn't know what was happening, we got off the bus in the Old Square Birmingham town centre. We were really rushing, I hadn't a clue what was going on.

We ended up in a building with loads of boots and shoes everywhere and that smell you get when in a shoe shop, but this smell was a different from a shoe shop smell you get today of course, it was leather then. I never forgot that smell. My mom handed the letter to the man. (WHY DID GROWN UPS LOOK SO STERN IN THOSE DAYS?) My mom sat me down took off my holy pumps (MY FOOTWEAR IN THOSE DAYS WAS VERY RELIGIOUS!) and socks; it was winter, I remember because my feet were wet and I had put on me a brand new pair of socks after drying my feet with her handkerchief. They felt so thick and warm with a pattern round the top, they were grey and to my surprise the man was trying boots on me; he tried two different sizes on me before saying, "Yes, these are alright." I asked, "Can I keep them on, Mom?" "Yes," she said, thanked the man and out we went.

Wow can you imagine not having to tuck your sock under your foot to put some space between your foot and the pavement because of the holes in your pumps and not have a soaking wet foot. I used to put cardboard in when the sock was so worn out and there wasn't enough material left to tuck under my foot but when wet it made my feet wetter plus it went all soggy and fell apart. When the weather was good the pavement rubbed it away to nothing in minutes. I walked out of that building with warm feet and legs but best of all I was walking with dry feet in the rain. I was so happy. I remember that day very well, it felt good. I now know the letter my teacher gave to me was for a free pair of boots and socks from that wonderful establishment known as the Birmingham Post and Mail. I believe they are also referred to as Daily Mail Boots. It turned out that a lot of children at school knew you had your free boots and socks by the socks; if you didn't wear the socks they couldn't tell. I believe the girls' shoes had eyelets in the sides of the shoe, which let other children know where the shoes had come from, and that they were free shoes.

Off to school one day feeling very warm and proud of my new boots, when two boys came up to me and very loudly said, "Free boots because your parents can't buy you any?" I answered with, "I had these yesterday, my mom bought them for me." "No she didn't you only get those socks when your parents have no money and you get them from the Birmingham Post and Mail, you are a scruffy scrounger, your parents don't look after you," they teased. I suffered many more comments from a lot of boys but more horrible comments from the girls. Well at least my feet were warm and dry.

WHITE MICE

The old market hall in Birmingham city centre, with large steps leading up into what to me looked a massive space with lots of traders selling so many different types of goods, was just like Aladdin's cave with all the traders shouting at the same time trying to attract the attention of the public as they passed their stall. This shell of a building with arches in the walls every few feet that were once windows made me walk round in awe of the place, and I seem to remember two big pillars either side of the steps at the entrance. I went on a Saturday with my friend Trevor to that old market place, we bought little white mice from there, 6d each (sixpence). Not being able to tell the difference between male and female I ended up with 23 white mice! I gave many of my friends that wanted to keep mice as many as they wanted, free of charge.

When I first started to collect mice, I said to the man selling them, "Mister, can I have that one?" He picked one up and with a deep breath and a puff and a few choice words he said, "Look, son, do you want this mouse or don't you?" "Yes, Mister," I said with a trembling voice. I got on the 14 bus to go home to Glebe Farm where I lived, and when on the bus upstairs I thought I would take a peep at my new little friend. I didn't know mice were so fast, and as soon as it saw the chink of light, it shot out of the box, ran up my arm, across my shoulders. I just managed to grab its tail, I think it didn't like that because it bit my finger and drew blood, so I threw him back in the box as quick as he came out. I won't do that again, I thought.

Back home I had a beautiful mouse box with a sliding glass lid, inside a well-made nesting box – I felt so proud, I had a factory-made mouse box, with a nesting box, little bowls for food and a bottle clipped to the side for water. In went the mouse, I felt so good I kept looking at it all night. (My mom said I couldn't keep it in the house in the day time.) Barry who lived next door gave me all the equipment and the mouse box, it was like Christmas come early, I covered it over with a waterproof canvas to keep him warm.

After a few weeks all was well, but one afternoon Barry's cat had slid the glass and got the mouse out before I could get to it, it was so badly cut I was in tears. I called Robert the neighbour who lived the other side of me, I asked, "Rob can you help?" "It's suffering, Dave," he said, "I can't kill it, Rob," I said. "I'll do it for you," he said, and threw it onto the concrete floor, "it's dead now," he said. I buried it in the garden and made a little cross for it. More errands to run, a couple of weeks later I bought another white mouse. I didn't open the box until I reached home, I had learned my lesson, this time I put half of a house brick on top of the box so the cat couldn't slide the glass.

Some time later I got another one just to give my first one a friend, and as I was cleaning them out a week later to my surprise there were 15 (talk about rabbits!). After cleaning them out I forgot to put the house brick back on the glass, the cat killed them one by one, he took them one at a time to his garden next door and they were scattered all round the lawn – he killed all 16. I just sat looking at all those baby mice lying on the grass next door, that was the end of me keeping pets. I shouted to Robert over the back fence, "Rob, do you want my cage?" "Yes please, Dave," he said, so I gave him every item I owned regarding the mice. "Why are you getting rid of them, Dave?" "It's the second time that cat has killed my mice, he won't kill any more of my mice because I won't have any for him to kill!" That surely did kill the pet-saving side of my life.

SHARE NUMBER

The Co-op (Co-operative Society), that was the shop that really fascinated me to the point where my imagination ran riot. My mom sent me to the Co-op many times over the years and I still went with her to buy items from this store. My mom would repeat, "Don't forget to give my share number," that number is burned into my brain 77467 – it rolls off the tongue like poetry. When I got married I could never remember our Co-op number, much to the annoyance of my wife, I gave my mom's number.

I remember those wires that went from the counter to the cash office upstairs, where there were two ladies that could be seen through big glass windows. The ladies serving on the shop floor weren't allowed to handle the cash in those days (it's hard to imagine that now isn't it?), they wrote down the cost of the groceries that had been purchased on a slip, the slip was then placed in what to me looked like a bomb, they screwed the cylinder with the slip inside it, to the lid of the cylinder which was on a wire. (I think that's how it went, my memory is fading a little!) The next operation really got my attention, after the lady had fixed it to the wire she pulled on a wire with a wooden handle attached to it, the bomb would travel upwards along the ceiling and straight in to the cash office, they would sort out the change then send it back to the ladies serving on the shop floor, with the slip and the change. They would call out the name of the person to give them their change, always the surname never by their Christian name, it's a shame they didn't leave it in the shop, people would go in just to look at it and of course spend while they were in there.

My mom saved up the dividend until Christmas if she could, which wasn't very often, as that time of her life things were very hard, the dividend book was black with hard covers, all entries in the book were done by hand when Mom did a withdrawal.

I was told if you want quality, shop at the Co-op; they were dearer than most so Mom rarely bought household goods from the Co-op, she had to settle for cheaper goods from other stores, as the old saying goes if you have only a 1/- (one shilling) you can't spend two.

SATURDAY PAY OUT

An occurrence that happened every Saturday morning that wasn't anything to do with me directly, indirectly maybe. Mother could not go out on a Saturday morning, that's the time when what we called club men came and club women in the main; it was men. Families where I lived, lived on the 'Glad and Sorry' so called because whatever you bought off those club men you paid every week a small amount of money until you had paid back all the cost of the items plus interest – that's why it's called the Glad and Sorry, Glad to have it, Sorry to have to pay for it.

Mother could only survive this way in life as most people did in those days – we had shoes, coats, bed linen, kitchen utensils, even paraffin heaters. Yes, if you were willing to pay weekly those club people were only too willing to sell it to you so you owed them that much money they kept you in debt for years so they could keep making profit off you. As the amount came down to almost nil this worried them so they would try very hard to tempt you to buy more items off them, they would even make believe they would reduce any item for you because you were a good customer but of course it was all over-priced to start with. Well, on the other hand if those firms had not been around most people would never been able to buy anything, it was no way to live but it was then the only way for my family.

Every Saturday we had Evans, S and U, Sloanes, the coalman, milkman, all calling for some money. To lessen the debt Mom would say to one of them, "I can't pay you this week," boy did they moan, she would say to another one, "I can only pay you 3d (three pence)." "Is that all, Mrs Prosser, it's not enough you know," they would say. I used to like the look on their faces when Mom would say to them, "OK, if you don't want it I will give it to Evans then." "No, I'll take it," they always answered. Mom did this balancing act with the few pennies she had; if she paid 2d or 3d to one, whichever one she missed she would give them double the week after and some weeks they were given nothing at all.

I've seen my mom in tears over club men pushing for money out of her. Mom always robbed Peter to pay Paul as the saying goes (the good old days, eh!), well they were the good old days for me but not for people like my mother who were trying to survive in this wonderful country we call England.

FARES PLEASE

Me and my sisters, we used to put the dining room chairs together in a row and pretending it was a bus, we would take it in turns to be the driver and the conductor. We did this many times in our young lives. My younger brother John was in his very early years at this time, my sister Doreen would sit him on her lap and make the engine noise to him and rock about to give the feel of the moving bus. My sister Janet would also do this for him. Of course as the years went by he sat on the chairs and make his own noises like an engine, as I did.

Sometimes, but not very often, my mom would go with my mate's mom Lizzie to have a quiet drink for an hour. As the saying goes, "while the cat's away the mice will play," that is so true. Our favourite game when no parents were around was to get a pillow and a blanket from the bed, put the blanket over the top stair, sit on the pillow and be pulled down the stairs. (No carpet in those days.) Well, it was great fun for us screaming and shouting, we drove our neighbours to the edge of despair, it must have been a nightmare to live next door to us. The next-door neighbour used to come round and be pulling his hair out. One particular evening we were playing tig and tag – you know, keep your feet off the ground, if touched by the one that's on when your feet were on the ground it was your turn to be on. The only difference this time we were doing it in the house running up and down the stairs, out the front door round the back through the back door shouting and I suppose making quite a lot of noise. My mom came in, shouted and told us to play more quietly – children play quiet? Not us lot, that's for sure, but because Mom was home we had calmed it down a little.

My mom, bless her, liked to see her children playing, she always said when she could see her children playing she knew we were happy. The next-door neighbour came round and banged on the door, my cheeky sister Doreen opened the door, the poor neighbour was so fed up he said, "I'm really fed up with you lot," and my sister smirking, "you will smirk on the other side of your face in a minute," then he said, "I suppose your mother is in the bloody pub again." My mom popped her head round the door and replied, "No she bloody well isn't!" A few words were exchanged! My mom's favourite saying then was, "got to play don't they, can't stop kids playing." Well, no way would I liked to have lived next door to a family as noisy as we were. Many years later when talking about it to my mom (the years fade the memories) I think she said, "You weren't that bad." Boy, if we weren't I would hate to live by children that were only half as bad as we were – we were very noisy, Mother!

PLAYING GAMES WITH BROTHER JOHN

As children do, my youngest brother John and I were playing tig around all three bedrooms – running, screaming, shouting, jumping all over the beds having a jolly good time. We hadn't any carpets in our house, only lino (that's short for linoleum) and every time we jumped off the bed on to the floor, well it sounded like thunder.

The next-door neighbours, we drove them spare; as we lived in a semi-detached house the floors were joined through the walls, so every time we jumped on the floorboards it sounded like we were in their house. They had four children, we never heard a peep out of them. As we were running from one room to the next, John still trying to tig me, I ran from Mom's room, to the little bedroom, John close behind me, I pushed the door to the closed position, John's big toe went under the door – his scream was deafening! It made a terrible mess of his toe and he was taken to hospital.

I got a good hiding, well-deserved I suppose, but we were only playing. He suffered a long time with that toe, in fact I took him some time ago to have that toe nail off at the foot clinic, maybe because of that accident all those years ago.

"LONESOME"

I came home from school one evening when I heard what I thought were the sounds of chicks; I looked in the cupboard at the side of the fireplace, and to my surprise they were all cuddled together, a dozen chicks. I was so excited, Mom told me Donald had brought them home. As a child does I kept picking them up, unfortunately one by one they died and only one remained – Mom named it "Lonesome". It grew big, and as it was growing up I noticed that every time I went by it, it pecked me, it pecked me even when I walked into the room and it was the same with my sisters. I played with it a lot while it was growing up, well one could say I tormented it I suppose, it must have been getting its own back.

Our mother was the only one that could do anything with it, never did it peck Mom. I could never go into the backyard without that chicken flying at me, I always ended up the line post screaming, "Mom, Mom, the chicken is pecking me." She would open the back door and shout, "Get in that pen now," (my eldest brother built the pen) the chicken stopped dead in its tracks, its head would go down and look at Mom, "I won't tell you again, get in that pen." It jumped down the two steps and very slowly it walked in to the pen.

"I hate that bird," I would say. Mom always said, "It's all right." Every day I would shout through the letter box, "Mom, is the chicken out?" Sometimes she didn't answer me, another time she said, "It's locked up," when it wasn't, and I would walk in – that silly bird would either chase me up the line post or into the outside loo. If it was the loo it walked up and down outside the door; there was a gap under the toilet door, and it would pop its head in the gap every now and again making a terrible noise to see if I was still there. I would be shouting at the top of my voice for ages calling, "Mom," when she finally came and locked the chicken up she would smile and say, "I forgot I had let it out." Every time I wanted to go in the backyard I would rattle the gate and shout, "I'm coming in," nothing, all quiet. Good, it's locked up, I thought, in I go. Just as I'm about to open the back door out would fly the chicken from behind the pen making a terrible noise pecking me all the way up the line post. It fooled me so many times to thinking it was locked up, it was a cunning bird, it did it to all my brothers and sisters that dared enter our backyard.

I shook the gate one afternoon from school, waiting to get attacked, when I noticed the chicken hanging over the drain, blood dripping from it. I thought at that time that was the happiest day of my life. In the living room Mom was crying her eyes out, "What's wrong Mom?" I asked. "My chicken is dead," she said. I'm not sorry, I thought, I hated it. My sister Kathleen told me on the 21st September 2009, when we were talking about that chicken and having a laugh, the reason Mom had its neck screwed was because it was egg-bound and suffering. When it was on my plate I sank my teeth into it, I felt like I was getting my own back. The girls, however, wouldn't eat it.

If you walked into our backyard as a child, this is where you would most likely end up shouting "Mrs Prosser, the chicken is pecking me."

NAILED

Whenever me and Trevor went to our park, we sometimes took a short cut down passages between the houses, much to the annoyance of the residents as those passages were for their use only – it was access for the dust men. At the end of the passage was a 6 foot fence; some children had broken a couple of the palings to gain access to the park, as the park entrance was at least a couple of hundred yards away we used those passages whenever we went to the tip or to play in the park.

This particular day we went to the tip; I suppose we were there about three hours looking for pram wheels and bicycle parts. On our way back to go up the passage someone had nailed a big board where the palings were missing. "Gosh," I said, "we now have to walk all that way to the entrance." I kicked the board in temper, and as I did it swung, "Ay, Trev," I said, "look at this." I was pushing it with my right foot and for some unknown reason enjoying it, what I didn't notice was the nail coming out. When it did finally come out the nail went straight through my kneecap and out the back of my knee. The weight of the board knocked me to the ground, for a few seconds I was panicking, as I sat wondering what to do. Trevor was more panicky than me, as the fear slowly left me I gathered my thoughts, I took hold of the board and as quick as I was able I pushed the board up and out came the nail – boy that was some pain, I can tell you. I rubbed my knee and limped home.

You know I never washed that wound or put anything on it, it was very sore the next morning. It healed up all on its own, never went septic, I never told my mom, don't think she could have taken much more of me and my antics.

TRAIN JOURNEY

One year I went with the school to Weston-super-Mare, it was a day trip; we saved 3d a week all year until we had paid enough (£1). Most times I ran errands to pay my 3d for this as my mother could never afford it, well now and again she would give me 2d, but in the main I ran errands and paid for myself. Sometimes, well most times, I would spend my money on going swimming or going to the pictures (cinema that is). On this occasion I was paid up, my mom gave me a one shilling piece, that's all I had. My clothes were washed and ironed; washing and ironing worn-out clothes didn't help them look good or much better, a little but at least they were clean and smelt nice. No children commented on my clothes, they were used to seeing me like that, they were all too excited to even bother I'm glad to say.

So we all gathered at the school, I only lived a few yards from the school, most of the parents were there to wave their little son or daughter off. I used to think how sissy it was to have your mom wave you off, dads were at work. Looking back I would have loved my mom to wave me off. We walked in file from Audley Road School, Glebe Farm, Birmingham 33 to Stechford Station; I loved that station – it was all wood, the wooden steps down to the platform were so wonderful to me.

I've loved station buildings and trains all my life. A lot of moms were there to wave off their little ones. I looked to see if my mom was there. Oh well, I was so excited anyway, a train journey was better than the seaside to me and my mind was on the fish and chips we were going to have at dinner time. We were all talking very loudly, full of energy, I remember they were all telling each other how much money they had to spend. Not one of them had less than a pound, one had £5. I was thinking, how can their moms afford that, I suppose I was thinking they were all as poor as we were but what a lot of money for a child in those days. Yes I was jealous, of course I was. I've thought about this a lot.

When we got to Weston it was a wonderful sunny day, and the station at Weston I loved it and (still do). We walked again in file to the beach, one exciting moment to see and smell the sea that looked to me the giant of a seafront.

What I've thought about all these years, all day long I was walking round Weston-super-Mare, I was on my own. I had no one to talk to – was it because I only had 1/- so I didn't have enough to go on the fair with them, or was it that they were so excited they just took off and couldn't wait to spend their money? As far as I know they were in twos or groups. I've never known why I was alone, could be other reasons. As I was walking round I hung on to my shilling.

We all met on the sea front and the teachers walked us to our dinner time restaurant upstairs to what I thought was a palace, the waitress came out with a beautiful plate of fish and chips. I was starving, it was a wonderful dinner then a nice cup of tea. Out we all went again and were told where we should all meet up at four o'clock, so in the afternoon I walked around again on my own.

Looking for a present for my mom with a shilling, I was hoping wasn't I? I looked in a shop where they were selling ice creams, and bought one for 6d. I thought with the 6d left I could buy my mom a present, whatever could I get for 6d for a present? There wasn't anything for a shilling, how or why I thought I could get her a present for 6d I've no idea. I started to feel quite guilty and ashamed, I had bought an ice cream but a 1/- or 6d would not have got a present for my mom.

Almost time to go and meet on the seafront, I had looked really hard for a present and no way could I get one, so I bought another ice cream with my 6d. I felt really sad I couldn't buy Mom anything. We arrived at the station, I was looking at all the iron work and the wood work on the station platform, it looked beautiful to me. I was in heaven, I do still love that side of life. On the train going back it wasn't quite as noisy as when we first got to the train in the morning, but still noisy; the noise ceased quite a lot I think after about half an hour. Then it went sort of quiet and they started to say what they had bought for their moms and dads. Some had bought statues, post cards, sticks of rock even novelties. I went nearer the window looking out of it, hoping no one would talk to me – they did of course, a girl with red hair, I've forgotten her name, said, "What did you buy for your mom and dad?" I'm sure I had a red face, "Nothing," I said, "I didn't have any money." "He hasn't bought his mom and dad a present, you are horrible, mean, did you hear that he spent all his money on himself and hasn't bought his mom and dad anything. You are selfish." Girls are so cruel at times, I felt terrible. "Well I've bought my mom and dad a present," she then pulled her tongue out at me and turned her back on me.

Suddenly we noticed we were approaching Stechford Station, there was pushing and shoving to look out of the window to see if they could see their moms. When the train stopped they all went for the door at the same time. There were moms and dads by the dozens it seemed. I stood out of the way. I heard such wonderful things said to the children by their parents, "Hello darling, hi sweetheart, I've missed you, oh it's good to see you, did you enjoy yourself?" Hugs and kisses, they even brought coats for their little ones. I waited to see if my mom was there, I knew she wouldn't be. All was quiet, I was standing on the platform on my own, I must confess a little tearful and I felt very lonely at that moment. I walked up those wooden stairs still hoping my mom would be there. Oh well, I thought, so I walked home alone.

I got to my house, not a soul was in sight. Boy I felt so unwanted (I was wanted of course, my mom loved me) but for a child to go through a day with all those people everywhere but me, I was alone. So I went round the corner to the British Legion which was just at the back of my house, I walked in (the doorman knew me), my family were there and just to end the day, worse than I thought possible, my mom held out her hand for a present. I think that moment was the lowest point of my young life.

That was the first time I went with the school to Weston-super-Mare. I went to Weston a couple of years after that, but once again I had only 2/- to spend. At least I had a day at the seaside which I was very grateful for, as I'm sure many children didn't have the opportunity to go.

OUR DUCK LONESOME

Again we had 10 or 12 chicks that we had in a cupboard next to the cast iron fire grate. Where they were purchased from I have no idea, my eldest brother Donald always got them. Any road up, one by one they died off, that used to sadden me, a few weeks later there was only one left. The difference being this one turned out to be a duck, it wanted to be the boss. A pen was built in the back yard the same place where that chicken Lonesome had its pen. Lonesome was that fierce hen that I wrote about in a previous chapter. This duck wasn't fierce, it did just what it wanted to do and again the only person that could control the duck just like that hen was my mother. Whatever she told it to do, it did. A little reluctantly sometimes but she always made sure it obeyed her.

Now who would have thought you could train a duck. Just proves that animals have brains and like us must be thinking. One day, so my mother told me and this happened a few times, she was walking up the road to the shops when she noticed people were laughing at her. Not being very well off and her clothes looking a little worse for wear, she was thinking that something must be wrong with her coat or (as she put it) her dress was tucked in her drawers. People would smile and say, "Hello, Mrs Prosser," for everyone in those days knew my mom. When my mom turned round to check her clothes were in order, there walking behind her was her duck following her up the road.

She told this story many times over the years, that's how I remember it so well. She would point her finger down the road saying, "Go home." The duck would turn its head and look at Mom who would say, "I won't tell you again, now get home." (That rings a lot of bells in my memory of my mom saying those very words to me over the years.) As the duck looked back at Mom it looked like it was saying, "Please let me come with you," just like me and my sisters used to say to her. We got the same response that the duck got from her. Off the duck went straight back home; it never wandered, it went straight into its pen. It's a wonder it was never attacked by any dogs because in those days dogs used to roam around free.

When I got home from school one evening just like that hen, Lonesome the duck was hanging over the drain with blood dripping from it. As I walked into the living room, Mom was sitting at the table crying her eyes out. When I asked her what was wrong she replied, "My lovely duck has gone." She cried the same when the hen had been killed. It is wrong to give any animal a name when you are going to eat it. That duck was really one of the family. We never had any more animals after the demise of that duck.

CIGARETTE CARDS

Jimmy, a boy me and my friends usually never played games with, he was very good at making a paper aeroplane – he threw it and it went round and round and round in circles, it was fantastic. I tried many times to fly paper planes, every time I tried to fly my plane it just nose-dived straight down.

Anyway, Jimmy had a biscuit tin full of cigarette cards that his granddad had given him. He would sell us some cards, about twelve cards for 3d (three pence) but he always insisted we played him skimmers so he had the chance to win them back. He always won them back, what we did would be to stand one card up the gutter and from the middle of the road we had to skim a cigarette card at the card standing up in the gutter and try to knock it down. The one who knocked it down won all the cards that had missed.

I never ever won him at this game and to my knowledge no one else ever did. Every time he knocked the card down he would shout, "JEN"– this was his favourite saying. We must have ruined some rare cards but of course they were worth next to nothing in those days.

BEING A ROUNDSBOY

At the top of my road a man named Arthur, a little wiry man with curly black hair, always wore a brown overall known as a "cow gown", this was because he delivered bread. He worked for a bakery company called Hardings Steam Bakers. At that time they had horses as well as petrol vans; I used to love seeing the horses being groomed and cleaned out. I even went to the boss who wore a white coat (that's what most of the bosses wore then) and asked if I could help with the horses. "You are too young, son," was his reply, "you aren't allowed by the horses at your age." I couldn't believe it. Sometimes when the men brought out the horses from the stables they would ask me to hold on to the reins for a short time which made me feel all grown-up.

Arthur drove a petrol van; one day when he was walking home I approached him and asked him, "Can I help you deliver your bread?" "OK," he said, "I leave the depot at 7.30 a.m." "OK, I'll be there," I answered. Great, I can earn money, but no wages were mentioned. I was there by 6.30 a.m. The face of the bus conductor when I asked for a 3d child's fare! It was just gone 6.00 a.m., and for a nine-year-old they thought I was just too young to be out at that time in the morning. I think it would be too early for a 65-year-old now. I walked into the bakery and was stopped by a man wearing a white coat, "What can we do for you, young man?" "I'm working with Arthur," I said. "Oh you mean Mo," the boss said. Funny, I thought, why do they keep calling him Mo when his name is Arthur? It was a few days later I asked one of the men tending the horses, "Why do you call Arthur Mo?" With a laugh he replied, "If at any time we call across the yard to him he always shouts back half a mo – Mo for short." "Oh," I said, not really understanding.

It's strange to think now, that then they allowed children around places like that at such a tender age. Being fascinated by the horses, time sort of flew by, when a stern voice said, "I've been waiting for you, if you don't buck your ideas up I won't let you help me again." It was Mo, I ran to the van, he lectured me all the way to the start of his round, saying I had made him late and I would have to run when delivering the bread to make up the time. Northfield and surrounding areas, we always stopped at the pub or should I say public house or boozers as my dad would refer to them. It seemed like an eternity waiting in the van, he was always over an hour in there every dinner time, he was a different person when he left the pub, I couldn't talk to him as I could before he went in there. When he had finished and completed the round he would pick a man up who worked on a building site, this man was also a neighbour, he only lived a few doors away from my house. I had to sit in the back of the van squeezed up against the bread trays (which were made of wire) and the back doors – that was the most uncomfortable ride I ever experienced, I was bounced about like a tennis ball. I only suffered it for three weeks, I didn't go again. He only paid me 1/- (a one shilling piece), it had cost me 1/3d (one shilling and three pence) in bus fares to travel there, so I used to walk home and the walk must have been five to eight miles. I'd had nothing to eat or drink, well to be honest I used to pinch the corners off the uncut loaves and hide a packet of morning coffee biscuits and eat them when he went into the pub and dispose of the wrapper down a drain in the road. I asked customers if I could use their toilet just so I could have a drink of water from their tap. Why did I stick it out for three weeks? – the promise of more money next time, but that never happened.

Milk rounds, I thought, so I asked the milkman if I could help him. He delivered all round the streets where I lived and paid me 1/6 (one shilling and six pence). Trouble was I'm a true Brummie and he was always telling me off for saying "bo-ul" instead of bottle, "nunk" for nothing, "gew" for going, "belly" for tummy. I got so afraid to speak so at weekends I helped the Corona pop man; their bottles in those days had a white porcelain stopper with a red rubber seal and this stopper was held down by a heavy duty wire that when pulled downwards tight to the neck of the bottle would seal the gas in which stopped the pop from spilling out. I enjoyed working for him, he gave me a bottle of pop and 2/- (two shillings) most times, 1/- (a one shilling piece) plus the bottle of pop. He insisted that when I helped him again I must return the bottle, there was a two pence deposit on the bottle. He was very kind to me and he said he liked me because I wasn't cheeky and I worked hard. One time I asked if my friend, Trevor could help him as well as me, "OK," he said, "but I will only pay you 9d (nine pence) each and you can share a bottle of pop." Great, I thought, me and Trevor, I know I got a little less money but Trevor was still my closest friend, we shared what we had anyway, in the week we ran errands, we always worked together and worked well. We helped the Corona pop man for a very long time.

One day a lorry was going slow; a young lad was running backwards and forwards to this lorry and he was leaving paper bags for old clothes to be put in, "Do you want any help?" me and a friend named Barry asked the man in the lorry. "OK, lads, I will pay you half a crown (2/6), and I'll be back in two days' time." We worked for two days delivering those bags to every house in the area. He did come back two days later, we met him at the top of the road and picked up all the bags filled with clothes, but at the end of the day he only paid us 1/- (a shilling) instead of half a crown. It seemed that children were always taken advantage of by adults. We had always worked very hard for our money.

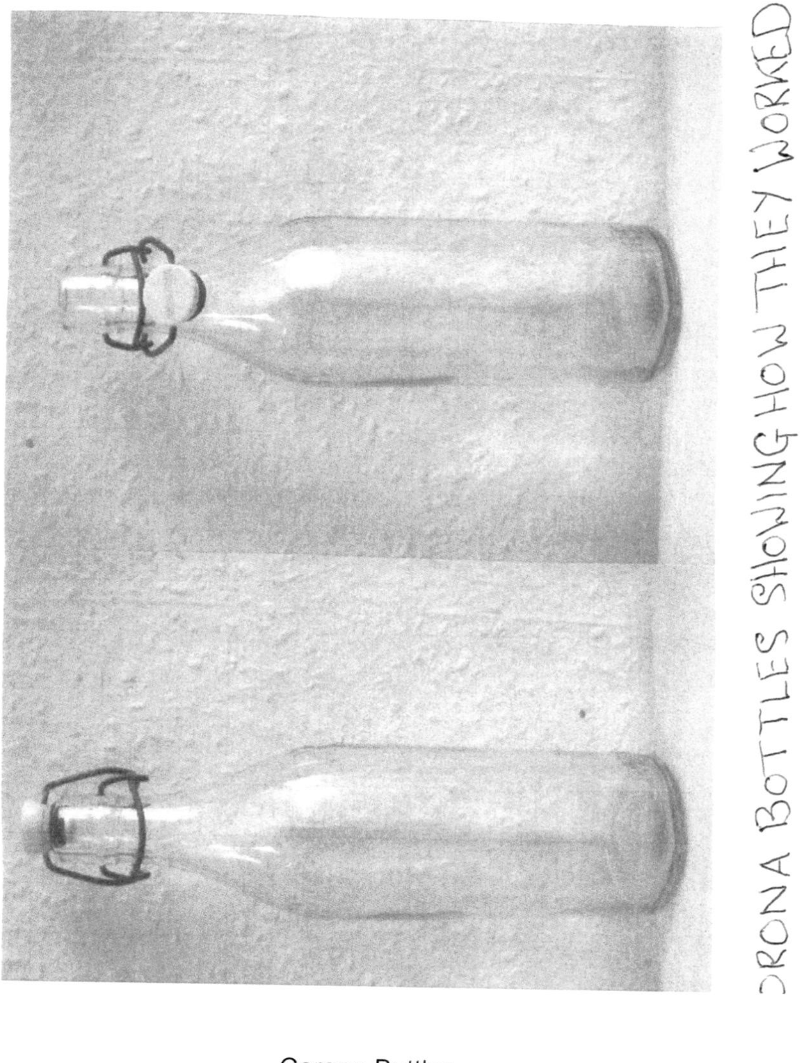

Corona Bottles

PAST DREAMS

I've been told thousands of times I shouldn't live in the past; I can't help it, poor as I was, knowing hunger, cold, living in well-worn clothes, hard work and running around in the snow until I could no longer stand, frozen fingers, soaking wet feet. I loved my childhood for the sunny days, playing, earning money. Cycling I really enjoyed, the warm days with my friends. I sit in the garden on a sunny day, feet up, close my eyes and remember my childhood days with my friends; on cold winter nights I do exactly the same. Lights out, glow from the fire (now of course it's a gas fire), feet up, all is quiet, nice and warm, my mind's eye goes all through my childhood days – that's how and why I remember so much. Things like my friend Trevor and his sisters used to go swimming with me and my sister Janet. We all ran errands to earn money for swimming. We even went scrumping apples together, not for devilment that was food to us. We did have our childish moments, like climbing over the railings into our school playground, climbing up the drainpipe and onto the roof; all the roofs were flat, and every time the caretaker with his two sons and an Alsatian dog would catch us and throw us out. Mind you, thinking about it, he was very good, he never once told the headmaster, we would have got the cane for sure.

Swancote Road, where Trevor lived, was a long road, eighty or ninety houses maybe more. One night, being a bit bored, four of us went to the top of the road ran, jumped, dived or rolled all the way to the bottom of the road over the gardens, we never trod or broke any plants down – mind you, most people didn't have flowers in their gardens just lawns. Yes every front garden, including Trevor's garden. Tying cotton to door knockers, pulling the cotton to knock the door and running away – most children did this I would think. Rolling little mud balls and throwing them at the windows or grit if we had no mud. Yes I was a normal child in that respect. I didn't annoy the neighbours very often. Me and my friends would play and enjoy life.

One memory that is very vivid in my mind, I lived in a corner house so from my back garden I could see a lot of back gardens in the next road, four back gardens from mine was a very big apple tree, it grew the biggest cooking apples I have ever seen. One night me and Trevor climbed over the hedges of the back gardens to this apple tree, we got two apples, must have been six inches across, sour but not that bad. Well, I could only eat half of this apple and Trevor only managed about the same. Next day we were walking down the road and the man whose apple tree it was called us over and shaking his finger at us said, "Don't you ever steal apples from my garden again," (I've no idea how he knew) "if you want an apple you knock at my door and ask for one." Not sure how many days went by, three or four, I knocked on his door and said, "You said if we wanted an apple to knock on your door and ask for one." Well he looked at me and Trevor and in total amazement he replied, "You cheeky little buggers," (lots of adults used that word then) "wait there." He came back with a big apple and said, "Half each and don't ask again," shaking his head as he closed the door, saying again to himself, "cheeky little buggers."

There are so many memories that come back when you sit quiet, close your eyes and start to think of your childhood. The good parts and the bad parts, the freedom I had as a child gave me much happiness.

THE RUBBISH TIP

As a young lad of 6 years I spent many hours on a rubbish tip behind the Atlas Cinema, Stechford, looking for shoes for my mom to burn on the fire. Also I was looking for old bicycles so I could take a tyre off one. A few weeks later I would find a wheel, pedals, chain, frame – it took months. I finally found a saddle with no covering on it, I was so pleased, I wrapped rag all round it so it could be sat on with some comfort. As a small boy I couldn't sit on the saddle and reach the pedals, no brakes on this bike and, oh yes, it was a girl's bike frame so I could stand on the pedals and with my arms up straight I could hold the handlebars. Down the hill I would go, I realise now my sense of balance was so good, very dangerous of course but as a youngster I knew no fear. (I used to jump off when I got to the bottom of the hill.) I ruined the clothes I had on (mind you they were worn out anyway) made worse with me enjoying my life as a youngster. Poor Mother, she used to get my clothes from jumble sales.

Anyway, there were not many cars about in those days, mostly horse-drawn carts, so down the hill with no brakes was quite safe car-wise. I had the surprise of my life one day finding an old bike on the tip, all rotten and bent up but brakes on it back and front; well I carried it back to a friend's house whose dad very kindly got the brakes off and saved one of the cables, he put the back brake on for me, I was so pleased, (what wonderful people in those days, always ready to help). It was a very long time before the front brake was fitted, I had that bike many years. Tyres, I always found them on the tip, worn but still OK, no frame just the wheel. I even found a wheel one day; a back wheel, complete tyre and cog in the river with air still in the inner tube, you know the sort that were usually punctured. I did change the girl's frame to a man's frame, a girl from school gave it to me, it had been left at the back of her shed, it was rusty but OK.

Trying to become a road user

We call these the good old days; I was very poor, shabby clothes but funny enough I was very happy when away from school hours and playing with my friends. GOOD OLD DAYS (Mmm, what do you think?). I always wanted better at the time. I was ridiculed, pushed around by teachers, had the mick taken out of me, tormented because I was scruffy but now I sit and think about those days with much fondness and wonder – was it so bad? Would I have liked to be better off, warm, well-fed and had a nice bike? YOU BET YOUR LIFE I WOULD. I did get a better saddle – yes, off the tip.

TEA UNDER THE APPLE TREE

Pype Hayes Park is a park near Erdington. My mom took me there, my little brother was in arms, only a baby. My mom's friend Winnie and her son John, my friend, we were there all day; our moms took sandwiches, bottles of water and a bottle of pop, no sweets or cake just sandwiches. We had a great day, me and my friend John. All there was in the park was a river, well a river to me was the nicest playground any child could ever want. I never went there again, only the once but the memories I have of that day will live with me forever.

The other place my mom took me to was a place called Sutton Park, we went there twice, none of my mates, it was just my mom my two sisters and my younger brother and me of course. What a big park, I remember walking for what seemed miles, there was a fair there; the twice I went with Mother there was a train running all round the outside of the fair. I had a ride on the train the first time I went. The second time my mom said, "Don't ask me for anything because I have no money." There is a stream there, I played in the stream all day. Whenever I went anywhere there was always a river to play in. I wonder do children do that sort of thing now?

One place my mom did take me was a place called Chelmsley Wood; there wasn't a river, there were lots of trees to climb, bushes to hide in, millions of bluebells to pick, lots of rhododendrons – it was a magic place to visit. One memory that will never fade about Chelmsley Wood is the first and only time I went with my mom – it was only Mom and me, where the rest of the family were I have no idea. We got on the bus at Glebe Farm, went through Kitts Green, then Lea Village and got off the bus at Tile Cross, walked towards Marston Green Village past a pub called The Bell, up a Road to the edge of Chelmsley Wood.

My mom brought me to Chelmsley Wood when it was all a wood. In the grounds there was an apple tree, we sat under the apple tree and the farmer's wife came out with a jug of tea, not a pot a jug and two cups and no saucers. Wonderful memories.

We walked along the edge of a field on the right was what was known then as the mental hospital, next to Marston Green Maternity Hospital. We walked along the path and at the end of it looking straight in front was a farmhouse, in its grounds was an apple tree. My mom told me to sit under the apple tree while she went to the house. She came back and sat down beside me, the sun was shining, a wonderful warm day, no one about, then what I suppose was the farmer's wife came out with two cups and a jug of tea. That's all I remember of that day, sitting under the apple tree with my mom and a jug of tea. I was very happy, that's why I remember that event so well.

Many a year later I tried to buy that farmhouse; I lived, would you believe, in the same road as that house and that apple tree was still there. I told my family every time we passed the house that I sat under that apple tree with my mom and had a jug of tea. The council bought the house and cut the apple tree down. I felt they had taken a little bit of me away.

TIDDLY WINKS

Coronation Day 1953, a magical time. I was very exited, tables all down the road, more food than I ever remember, so much sweet stuff, everyone laughing, smiling – a very happy place to be. I lived in Plowden Road, Glebe Farm, Birmingham 33. They had tables for Plowden Road at the top of the hill. I was sitting at a table in Swancote Road, all my friends came from Swancote Road. I really should have been in my road but I wasn't and I have never known why.

Trevor's mom Lizzie, who was my mom's best friend and lived in Swancote Road, squeezed me in. My friends all had a dickey bow tie that lit up and I had nothing, yes I was jealous. I felt left out. I was wondering why everyone had something and I and my sisters and younger brother had nothing, present wise that is. I made a pig of myself with the food and yet when the people from Plowden Road went to my school for the games, all my family were there, we were all dressed up for the fancy dress, my eldest sisters Kathleen and Doreen made our costumes out of crepe paper. My younger sister was the Queen of Hearts, I was a clown (I was always told I was a clown by my mom, that's the reason I was dressed up as a clown), my youngest brother was dressed up as Little Red Riding Hood, as you can see us in the photograph.

We didn't win the fancy dress. When it came to the games I entered for the running because I was fast, I thought if I win please don't give me Tiddly Winks, I hate that game (I still do). I was hoping for a gun or a car, but no, what did I win? You've guessed it – the Tiddly Winks. My sister and little brother played with the game but not me.

Coronation Day, 2nd June 1953, author's family from left to right:
Back row Kathleen, Dad, Doreen, Mom,
Janet as the Queen of Hearts, John as Little Red Riding Hood,
author David as a clown.
The costumes were made by my two sisters, Kathleen and Doreen
for the fancy dress parade, out of crepe paper.

Street Party
Neighbours and friends of Plowden Road, Glebe Farm, outside Audley Road School.

We had a big bonfire in the middle of the road, this also was to do with the Coronation; I remember going round all the houses in my road to get any item they were throwing away for the bonfire – 78 records, sideboards, chairs, trees, old timber, I collected all sorts of things even toys. I went to one house where the man said, "Hang on a minute, I'll look in my shed." What a shock – he came out with a rocking horse. He saw the look on my face, he then said, "No, I will put it on the bonfire, if I give it you, you will take it home and give it to your little brother." That's exactly what I was thinking and he knew it. My little brother would have loved it. I was very disappointed.

The bonfire was to celebrate the Coronation, the fire was in the middle of the road which was shaped like a circle which led to a grove, so lots of room. On the night when they lit the fire there was so much furniture, I wonder how many would-be antiques were burned that day all over England.

Fireworks, it was a wonderful time, even potatoes were roasted in the hot embers; while I'm standing there, I noticed the rocking horse burning – what a shame, my brother could have had so much fun on that horse. When we were playing games at my school we all grouped together for a photograph. I still have photos of that day, with me dressed in crepe paper as a clown.

Wonderful time, wonderful memories.

THE CORN SHOP

In our house we as children were disciplined by our mom, she ruled with a rod of iron, never our dad. Mom was the driving force. Off our kitchen was the coal house – that's where Mom kept the cane; knowing it was there made me think twice before doing anything wrong. I still got out of line sometimes, then Mom would say "coal house." "Sorry, Mom," I would say. "If I have to tell you again you will get double three whacks across the backside," kept me in check, I needed that discipline, I was a little rogue. I always knew when my mom was angry, she always folded her arms in an austere way, I knew that was it. After I was caned I always had to put the cane back in the coalhouse. When I walked back in she would kiss me on the forehead and say, "Now be a good boy."

I had the bright idea that if I broke up the cane she would not be able to use it, so one day while she was out at the shops I broke it up and put it in the dustbin. The next day while playing in the road with Trevor, my mom called me into the house and asked me to go to the corn shop, "Here is three pence, go and buy me a nice thin cane, one with a nice thin end."

The corn shop was called Turners, they sold corn, fertilisers, pigeon food, sacks of oats – I used to buy these many times for our family to eat for breakfast. There used to be mice droppings in these oats! A scoop was used to measure the oats into a brown paper bag. This scoop was used for all the animal food, but the person serving did not know they were being eaten by my family and probably other families in the same position as ourselves. So I looked for the finest cane I could find, being very particular about the one I chose, I shook the cane to make sure it had a really good whooshing sound, gave the money to the man wearing his brown cow gown that I had always seen him wear as far back as I could remember.

Walking back down the road I thought, my mom will love this – talk about being thick! Into the house I go, “Here you are, Mom, I picked the best one,” I said, and with that Mother bent me over and really gave me six of the best. Hurting, crying and very bewildered I asked her what she had hit me for and told her I had been a good boy. She said, “You broke the cane up and put it in the dustbin and thought I wouldn’t see it didn’t you, now you can put this cane in the coalhouse,” always referred to as the “coal ole”. So out to play I went with a backside ringing and stinging. If only I had covered the cane up when I put it in the dustbin, maybe I could have saved all that pain?

MAKING SLIDES

A very cold winter's day I was playing in the horse road, it was covered in deep snow. All my friends were out playing, it was very cold, in fact it was well below freezing, so we got buckets of water and poured it in the middle of the road the night before. My road was quite a steep hill, we started the slide just outside my house, the slide ran to the bottom of my road, across Swancote Road that ran across the bottom of my road over the pavement and to the garden hedge of our friend Rita Hill. The slide must have been 110 yards long. We all started to slide down the hill across the road, at the bottom the snow was so deep we catapulted over the hedge into a garden at the end of the slide.

The snow in the garden must have been 5ft deep, maybe even more. I remember the hedge next door was very high, the snow in that garden was even deeper. Me being the smallest, skinniest kid of them all, I was constantly thrown over the hedge. As the snow had never been walked on I landed in the snow and was buried. I disappeared and found that to be very frightening, at first all the lads had a very good laugh at my expense. This was made worse when the girls came out to play as lads do. I think lads are born to show off in front of girls. I went over the hedge quite a few times. I was by this time very wet and frozen and feeling very uncomfortable. The girls were very wrapped up, wellingtons, hats, scarves and gloves. The boys never wore scarves like the girls did. Me, I was in short trousers, shirt and a coat, socks with more holes than material (I used to tuck them under my foot, which meant they couldn't be pulled up) and of course pumps with holes in and no gloves. I was enjoying life playing with my friends. Trevor was dressed the same as I was, as he was as poor as me. The lads, of course still showing off around the girls, pulled off my pumps and my worn-out socks held them up in the air and shouted, "Hey, girls, do you want a pair of socks like these!" That was vey embarrassing to see the girls laughing at me.

With all the sliding the ice became like glass, and when the baker came down the hill with his horse and cart, the horse started to slide down the hill. I was so worried for that horse I cried, thinking it was going to hurt itself. The cart went sideways and pulled the horse away from the icy slide. The deep snow in the road brought the cart to a halt. I was so relieved my nerves were on edge. From that day to this it made me respect horses. In the house I go to try and get dry and warm. My mom asked me to run up the road to the shops. She always said run. I was cold and wet standing by the fire, I just didn't want to move so I said "Mom, I'm cold," I didn't want to go to the shops. My mom was a large lady so she put her coat and said, "Oh I'll go myself, it'll be quicker." As she walked across the road she stepped onto our slide fell over and hurt herself quite badly. I felt very guilty, and with tears in my eyes I said, "I will go the shop." She was laid up for about two weeks after that fall. Whenever she asked me to run up the road after that, I did.

That same winter me and Trevor made good money shovelling snow from paths. I never liked shovelling snow and still don't. There were six of us lads all together, but it was only ever me and Trevor that tried to earn money as they all got pocket money but me and Trevor didn't until we were much older. This was because my dad was a very heavy drinker and didn't like parting with his money. All the pubs that my dad drank in have now been demolished. (I often wonder if it's because my dad stopped drinking there!)

WHITE WINTER

IT WAS WINTER AND I WAS SMALL,
NO UNDERWEAR HAD I, NO NONE AT ALL,
THE CLOTHES I HAD WERE IN POOR SHAPE,
I PLAYED IN THE SNOW AND THOUGHT THIS IS GREAT,
NOT FOR LONG FOR I GOT COLD,
I WAS ONLY A CHILD AND NOT VERY OLD,
ALL MY SCHOOL DAYS WERE LIKE THIS,
CHILDREN LOVED TO TAKE THE MICK,
NO WELLIES ALL MY YOUNG LIFE,
HOLES IN MY PUMPS, WELL THAT'S LIFE,
PUMPS IN THE SNOW WELL WE WERE POOR,
THAT WAS MY LIFE, THAT'S FOR SURE.

LAND OF THE SPITFIRE

Castle Bromwich Aerodrome used to have open days, how often I'm not sure. Out front on a stand used to be a Spitfire. I loved going there, to a young lad these places were captivating. I always went there with Trevor's brother Tony, I never remember Trevor going.

The one thing that has stuck in my mind was a long glass case with hedges, building and a bell on the bottom in the middle of the scenery. The object of the exercise was to release the bomb from underneath the plane, with finger 'on the button the plane came along. When the button was pressed the bomb would fall and you had to hit the bell. After a few goes, I hit the bell every time. The RAF man said, "You are too good now," and stopped me using it.

It was great fun. I watched the paratroopers jumping out of a barrage balloon. I loved to see those big parachutes open, they are bigger than they look when they are on the ground. I didn't know at the time that my wife's uncle was a paratrooper and I watched him jump out of a balloon. Next open day I couldn't wait to have a go on the display model. I went in and said to all the boys there, "I can hit the bell every time." When my turn came I said, "Watch this, I never miss." Well, I couldn't get near the bell, not once did I hit it. Serves me right for being so big-headed. That day taught me a good lesson.

SNOW HILL STATION

Trains are one of the loves of my life. There were two stations I really loved, both were in Birmingham – one I've so many fond memories of one was Snow Hill and the other was Stechford Station; both stations are still in use but alas both were knocked down and rebuilt, nowhere near as good as they were before. The old timber and stone work to me were majestic.

One wonderful memory I have of Snow Hill Station is a stamping machine – green in colour with a big brass arrow in the centre of it and the alphabet all round the outside. When I turned the arrow to each letter in turn and pulled a big lever on the side of the machine it stamped out the letter that had been selected. Me and my friend Trevor printed our name out on that machine every time we went to that wonderful station, it only cost a penny a go and it came out stamped on a strip of aluminium. We always bought a penny platform ticket and were thrown out of that station more times than I care to remember by one of the porters, for no other reason than we were kids. Never playing up, we always said the same thing, "We have a platform ticket, mister." They always said the same thing to us, "I don't care, out you go," that was the normal reply we got on that concourse.

I was in heaven, the smell of the locos, I can smell it now can't you? If only they could bottle it, all train enthusiasts like myself would buy a gallon. I adored seeing the trains coming and going it was a thrill for me to see the motion of the wheels and the valve gear all moving together, to be honest I still get a kick out of it. The day they started to knock Snow Hill Station down I had a tear in my eye, I can tell you; that was a massive loss to the people of Birmingham, we lost a beautiful masterpiece and I just cannot bring myself to go and look at that modern rebuild. I will live on my memories the original station will live in my mind's eye for ever.

IN AWE

Every day Trevor and I went into town we headed for Snow Hill Station. Every time I think of that beautiful station I can never understand why they would wish to destroy what was an icon in the railway world. That station was worth more than money, and I miss that stamping machine.

Trevor and I always liked to walk around the market, one of my favourite places was Nelson's column by St Martins church, watching the escape artists trying to escape from the chains they were bound in. The blind lady always fascinated me shouting "handy carriers", she was there for years and I was privileged to buy a carrier from that lady for my mom a time or two – God bless her.

If we had any money we always made a bee line for the man selling baked potatoes, 6d a spud, he always used those white cone-shaped paper bags, same as the ones they used in sweet shops when you bought 2oz of sweets. He always put salt in the bottom of the bag and the spud on the top; we loved buying those spuds in the winter time, it was great to stand next to the oven and feel the heat from it on a cold Saturday morning. One Saturday we went to see him he said, "Hello, boys, nice to see you again – do you want a potato?" "We only have 3d each," I said. I was expecting him to shout, I'd had my share of being shouted at I can tell you, no me and Trevor were never cheeky. "OK, boys, a small one for 3d."

FAITHFUL FRIENDS

Our dog Rex was a what my mom would call Heinz varieties, he was a cross between I think a Jack Russell and anyone's guess. White all over except for a brown patch on the middle of his back, we went everywhere together, we were pups together. Rex was a very loyal dog.

One day me and my friends were walking to Saltley when they decided we should catch the bus, I forgot my dog Rex was with us, Tony said, "You forgot your dog." I felt really bad that I had forgotten him, boy did he run fast. I was calling him, "Come on Rex, come on boy," he jumped on the platform of the bus and I was so relieved. I took him upstairs, all my friends made a fuss of him, he loved it, he licked their faces until they looked clean. Where we were going, I'm not sure, I remember that part of the day because I felt so bad about Rex, leaving him when I caught the bus.

A long time after that I was round at the shops where I grew up; in the evening we usually walked around the shops or sat on the wall of the Glebe pub, (this was at Glebe Farm, Stechford), when a boy came up to us, me and Trevor that is. I knew the boy by sight because he went to our school, he lived a few yards away from the pub. He asked us, "What are you doing round here?" "Nothing," we replied. "Clear off," he said, "this is my area, not yours." "I will go where I like, you can't stop me," I replied, then he went to punch me. Rex, from a standstill, flew at the boy and grabbed his arm – well I was so surprised, I never knew my dog would protect me like that. I was so proud of him, the boy backing away from us was whimpering with fear. "Come here Rex, good dog," I said, making a fuss of him.

The boy was running away shouting, "I will fetch my big brother to you." I proudly shouted back, "Yeah, I will set my dog on him." I was so shocked my dog had saved me from a beating up. About five minutes later I saw the boy with his big brother, he looked really angry, I was scared stiff of this big brother I can tell you. "Is that them with that dog?" I heard him say. "Yes," the younger boy said. The older boy went to punch me and again my dog Rex flew at him, well I could not believe how scared of my dog he was. As the dog went for him he half turned in fear. Well I saw something you only see in cartoons because Rex missed his arm and caught the back of his trousers, well the boy was spinning round in circles with the dog outstretched going round and round. This big boy was whimpering louder than his little brother had, who was now running down the road so fast he nearly fell over. The dog gave up his grip and came running to me. The big boy was so scared, as he was running away he was shouting, "I will get the police, they will have your dog put down." Brave boys soon became cowards when faced with a growling dog. I never heard any more about the incident, it never happened again, it made me love that dog for all time.

Funny really, I have a terrible fear of dogs. That dog lived with us for many years, the only food he ate was what we left on our plates. We fed him biscuits, cake, (not often as those two items we only had on rare occasions) bits of chocolate at Easter, in fact no matter what it was Rex would eat it, no fancy tinned dog food in our house – ha, if there had been I think for sure we would have eaten it.

One evening when school was finished for the day, I walked into the kitchen of my house when I heard a loud sobbing noise. Into the living room I go in a hurry, my mom was sitting at the table sobbing her heart out. "What's the matter?" I asked. My dog was dead, I was told – oh no, my Rex. We had one car a week or fortnight down our road and it seems Rex saw a cat run across the road straight under the car, this is what the man told my mom. He very kindly carried Rex and put him in our back garden, I dug a hole in the front garden and buried him there.

It's a shame I haven't one photograph of Rex, our faithful dog, but he gave me many happy memories.

Those bullies were not as tough as they thought they were when confronted with my dog Rex.

BUTTERFLIES

At the back of my house was a big hole, I used to catch newts there. I was told by one of the boys that used to use the hole as a scrambling circuit that the hole was made by a bomb, he would ride his motorbike in and around that hole. I was always worried he would hurt the newts. Years later the hole was filled in and they built a British Legion on the ground, since then that building has been demolished, now lots of houses stand there.

Before all those changes took place when it was a big hole with newts breeding in it I also caught butterflies there. I was chasing a beautiful coloured butterfly with a net made from one of my mom's old stockings tied to the end of a twig, the stocking kept coming off so I held the stocking at the end of the stick so it wouldn't come off anymore. I caught two butterflies, then I spotted a Bob Howler as we called them. I ran to try to net it, tripped and badly cut my left wrist right down to the bone – off to the hospital, four stitches.

I did make my mom's life hard. SORRY MOM!

FLYING HIGH

Model aircraft was not a great love of mine, I liked them, OK, but trains were the love of my life. After running errands one week I did really well, so I went up town to a model shop in Temple Row, opposite St Phillips church in Birmingham city centre. I loved that model shop, there were aeroplanes hanging from the ceiling and other made-up kits, it truly was an Aladdin's cave. I used to go in to that shop just to look around. I purchased a Tiger Moth aircraft kit, it was all in Balsa wood, I can't remember the cost of it. I hurried home with visions of flying it in four days' time.

What prompted me into buying an aeroplane kit was as I was walking up the road to our shops a boy came out of his house with a model of a Hurricane that was beautifully painted. Trevor was with me, we walked over to the boy and asked him what the plane was called. He told us he had only finished it that morning, "You can look at it but no touching," he had put an engine in it and with a flick of the propeller it started. What a row it made for a tiny engine! We walked down the park with him, he started the engine off – cor I thought, I want one of those. The boy said, "If you are really interested I will show you how to put them together and dope them," that was a new word to me and Trevor. He got some tissue and pasted the dope on it, that's what you do, then you place it over the frame of the aircraft. He said, "It goes taught when it dries like this," and showed us an unpainted one. It's really amazing how taught it goes.

Did I say flying in four days? Well it looked easy when that boy was showing me. I was trying to study the plans but not being very bright I just could not work it out. A couple of days later I must try, I thought to myself, so I laid out the plans and tried to glue all the struts together for the wings. I glued them to the plans, I broke some struts, some got twisted, that was the end of that plane. I was wishing dad would guide me but no such luck.

A couple of years later I did buy another one but I made the same mistakes again, that kit never got past one wing, it too ended up in the dustbin.

What I needed was an adult's guiding hand but it never happened; trouble as well was I didn't have any craft tools, I only had my mom's carving knife. Talk about doing everything with nothing, but I couldn't have done it even if I had everything.

The flying game, never to be.
Attempting to make a Balsa wood bi-plane.

BACK GARDEN ADVENTURE

Billy, the boy who lived in Swancote Road (he's the one that fell off the scaffold of Kenilworth castle) lived with his granddad, mom, dad and sister. He was better off than all the rest of us put together – he had a tandem bike, trolley, tent, games, good clothes, binoculars. He was a wiry little fellow. One day he said to me and Trevor, "I've got my tent up in the back garden, come down tonight you can sleep in it." It was the old green thick canvass type. Off we went at eleven o'clock on the night. I told my mom, "I'm sleeping in Billy's room tonight." She didn't mind, she just said, "You behave yourselves."

We waited for Billy to enter. How he got out of his house without his mom or dad knowing – he climbed out of his bedroom window, slid down the drainpipe and let us in the backyard. Being in the summer it wasn't total darkness. Billy had a torch with him to guide us right across the yard where there was a shed dividing the yard from the garden where Billy had his tent. As he led us through the entrance there was a shed either side. Out in the back garden we slept in that tent all night, it was quite an adventure.

The next morning after his mom and dad went to work Billy came to see how we had liked our stay. "Great," we said. "Good," said Billy, "any time you want to drift in again just let us know." We never did stay there again; when we told the other lads they all said they had done that a few times. I myself only did it once. Great memories of doing those sorts of things. As we walked through the sort of archway or covered way, Billy opened the shed to get his bike out and there in all its glory was the oldest motorbike I had ever seen at that time. It was in beautiful condition. I asked, "What's in the other shed?" When he opened the door it was like Aladdin's cave – tools hanging up, what a wonderful workshop. No wonder then whoever it was made Billy's trolley made a fantastic job. He also had stilts. I always wished at that time I could have all those things. But when I got anything I adored it and loved it whatever it was. Billy loved all of his possessions. I wouldn't think he had quite the feelings I got when I acquired anything, when things are got easy. I don't think it's possible to have the same feelings as earning and working hard for them, I may be wrong. What do you think?

That motorbike I saw in Billy's shed ended up in the motorbike museum at Bickenhilll, across the road from Birmingham International Airport.

SCHOOL HOLIDAYS

One day in the 6 weeks school holidays I went to the tip, I could not believe my eyes – there in all its glory was the bottom half of a pushchair, all four wheels were there and in good condition; being a pushchair and not a pram the wheels were the small type and not the big ones. I was so excited to see those wheels they were like gold, they were never thrown away not in the 1940s, people always made use of wheels in those days and never ever threw them on a rubbish tip, they were always used to make carts for fetching coal and taking rubbish to the tip. Any road up, I picked up the frame with the wheels still attached and ran all the way home, the reason I didn't try taking the wheels off at the tip was I was afraid some bully boy would take them off me. Oh yes, there were those types around even in those days, I had my share of being bullied by older boys, I was a tough little fellow and strong but I was a placid boy, I hated arguing and fighting so I did neither, I like the peaceful life.

When I reached home I set to and started to clean the wheels, I love things to be clean – after saying that, can you imagine the state I was in! Oh yes, in a state alright, but at that moment in time I didn't care, I was the king of our street, I had four wheels plus the axles. Right, I thought, now all I need is a plank and two pieces of wood to fit on top of the axles so I kept going to the tip. It was about six weeks before I found a plank, the one I found was four feet long one and a quarter inch thick, ten inches wide if my memory serves me right. After finding the plank I needed lots of nails, so back to the tip several more times to find the nails I required. I found half a house brick which I used to get the nails out of the wood – I found that with my hands pushing the nails back and forwards I eventually got the nails out; it took me days to get the amount of nails I needed, but I did get extra just in case I needed them. With a pocket full of rusty nails I walked home; the nails were in my trouser pocket which was the only place I could carry them, every time I went to the tip, as I hadn't a coat at that time (did you know a boy with half a house brick and a piece of wood can demolish a house HA HA!).

I straightened all the nails in my back yard with my half a house brick, well I hadn't got a hammer. I nailed the two pieces of wood to the axles, I then nailed the axle to the back of the plank and the front – boy was I proud I was now the owner of a trolley, I was so pleased with myself. Ah string, I thought, yeah my mom's washing line, lots of spare wrapped round the line post because it was too long, so I went and found Mom's scissors and I helped myself to a long length of it. (I got a good hiding for cutting the washing line.) I tied it to the front axle, just the job, and pulled my trolley up to the shops.

The first shop was called Stockton's, it was our local newsagent; outside of this shop was a good slope so I pulled my trolley right to the front door of the shop, sat on it – away I went. This is great, I thought, down the slope I've got to turn the front wheels, they won't turn! What do I do now? So I pulled hard on the rope to turn left, and as I did the front axle came off. I went flying, grazed my knee, and as I sat on the pavement rubbing my leg, a man walked past and asked me what had happened, "My front wheels have come off," I explained. "What you need, son, is a nut and bolt, if you make a hole through the plank and the axle, put in the bolt then you will be able to turn the front wheels." "Thank you, mister," I said. What a nice man, I thought, he didn't laugh at me or ridicule me like everyone else does, what a fool I am, I said to myself, of course I need a nut and bolt.

I carried my trolley home, got my mom's poker from the fireplace, lit the gas stove, put the poker into the flames till it glowed red hot (I saw my dad make holes this way), I then burned a hole in the plank. This took three goes before I got a hole through the plank and a further three times to get a hole through the wood on the axle. I knew my mom was short of money so I put three pennies in the gas meter, she never knew I did it, she couldn't understand how she got so much gas for her one penny.

When my dad came home from work I asked him if he could get me a nut and bolt from work, when I showed him what I wanted it for he was so proud of me, "Did you do this all on your own?" "Yes," I replied. With a pat on the head he said, "Well done, son." I felt very proud, he had never praised me up before, "I will get your nut and bolt tomorrow," he said.

The next evening I fitted the nut and bolt that my dad gave me, and up to the shops I go, outside the newsagent's shop doorway sat on the trolley, down I rolled, pulled on the rope to turn left, round I went. It felt great, I was really excited. My friend Trevor saw me, "Cor, Dave," he said, "whose is the trolley?" "Mine, Trev," I answered, "I made it all from the tip when you weren't with me, thought I would surprise you." "Let me have a go, Dave," Trevor asked. "OK, Trev, don't crash it." He loved it, I got quite a big head, well I had never done anything before. The next afternoon all my friends had a go on it and my other friend Billy said, "My dad has made me one, I'll go and get it." "We can have a race," I said to him. Billy laughed at me and said, "What – you race me on that old wreck?" "Yeah, come on, Billy," they all shouted, "OK, OK, I'll go and get it."

Well when I saw his trolley my heart sank I can tell you, it was painted green and red with a padded seat and white lining all round it, I thought it was beautiful, all my mates were laughing at me by this time, "Well you threw out the challenge," said Eddie." "It's OK," I said, "you never know I might beat him." Well that gave them another good laugh, I was dying inside with shame as we both sat on our trolleys, Billy sat high on his trolley he had big pram wheels on the back, small ones on the front, I only had small wheels all round, his small wheels where bigger than mine. As we sat on our trolleys a young girl walked past, Billy said. "Ay love, he has challenged me to a race – who do you think will win?" I felt my face go red, "Oh yours will easily," she said. "See, Dave," he said, "I told you." I said, "OK, Bill, a rolling start no pushing."

Beating Billy downhill on my trolley that I had made up from the tip made me feel very good.

Off we went and to my surprise and delight downhill I was much faster, not until we hit the flat did he pass me, "That was a fluke," he shouted, "let's do it again." We did a further four times and I was much quicker downhill so I shouted, "I'm king of the hill!" I felt great, Billy had a posh trolley made by his dad, mine was made up from scrap, off the tip and cost me nothing, that taught me never to judge a book by its cover. I had years of fun on that trolley and do you know for the life of me I can't remember what happened to it.

THE RIVER BLYTHE

Coleshill, a little village in North Warwickshire, the first time I ever went there was with my next-door neighbour Barry. My mom took me there once, I went on the bus with her, then a couple of years later I went to the same spot with my mates on a bike I had made up from the rubbish tip. It seemed like there were hundreds of people walking down Maxstoke Lane to the same spot, all it was, was a field with a river running through it; this field was at the bottom of a steep hill, people were having picnics there, children paddling, me and my mates went there to swim. There was a little white cottage known as Cuttle Cottage, the field was Cuttle meadow and the little bridge over the river was Cuttle bridge. Opposite the cottage was a wooden shed that had been turned into a tea hut, that's all there was, a lot of the time the tea hut wasn't open. One hot day we were getting a cup of tea from the hut when Billy went to the dustbin at the side of the hut, picked up a stone and started to kill the bees that were buzzing round the bin, when he suddenly jumped up screaming – a bee had stung him on the lip. Boy, within seconds his face had swollen up like a balloon.

I never took a towel to dry myself with, I used to run around till I got dry. One very hot afternoon a man came up to me and asked if I would sell him my swimming trunks, "No," I told him, "I will give you half a crown (2/6d)," he said. I was tempted. "All right, five bob (5/-)," he said. I answered with, "They won't fit you." "Yes they will," he replied, "they tie at the sides, OK 7/6 (seven shillings and six pence)," that was a fortune to me. "OK," I said, so with Johnnie's towel wrapped round me I took off my trunks. He gave me the 7/6d and without a care he undressed without covering himself, to say they fitted where they touched is an understatement, he was happy and so was I.

A day at Coleshill. We used to swim in this river (the River Blythe). The cottage is Cuttle Cottage in the meadow known a Cuttle Meadow. The bridge over the river is also called Cuttle.

I was telling Robert who lived next door, his house was joined on to my house, about the field in Coleshill. "I want to go," he said. "Your dad won't let you," I said. "I won't tell him, Dave, I will take my tent if you let me go with you." "OK," I said. So without his dad seeing, he passed his tent over the fence to me and I tied it onto the back of my bike.

Next morning I met Robert round the corner, he sat on the crossbar, off we went. It was a struggle, we kept changing over so we had a break from the pedalling, we got there OK. Robert was loving it, nice warm day, when to my surprise my mom turned up with Johnnie's mom. It started to rain so my mom and Johnnie's mom went into Robert's tent, poor Robert stood outside getting wet, he wasn't very happy.

The rain stopped, the sun came out, we had a great time. I took Robert a couple of times after that but without the tent. As I was swimming against the current Billy, who always played up, picked up a dried cow pat and threw it quite hard; it hit just below the shoulder blades and took all the wind out of me, plus it felt like a thousand injections. I was fighting to stop going under, I swallowed a fair amount of water. I nearly gave up when I felt the bottom of the river bed, I stood up emptying my lungs of water, Billy was on the bank laughing his head off. We never fell out.

My mom always said "These young days are the best days of your life, young man." How right she was.

GAS WORKS

Trevor came to me one day, he said, "Dave, Mrs D. wants a quarter hundred weight of coal." We went to Whites coal yard in Church Lane, Stechford, in all weathers, we would carry coal – wind, snow, rain, frost, nothing stopped me and Trevor from earning money; we got 3d sometimes 6d (sixpence), in snow we always got 6d. Mrs D gave us a shilling (1/-), that was a lot of money to us. We never had a wheelbarrow, I used to carry it while Trevor held it at the back. I asked him recently if he did ever hold it to help take the weight of my back, he said, "No I didn't." No wonder my muscles got bigger! I am 66 now, Trevor is 67; we always reminisce about our young days and the things we did to make a penny. When I was carrying the coal I carried it till it got too heavy for me, I used to drop it, have a rest for ten minutes then ask a man that was passing to put it on my back. I got comments like: "it will kill you," or "it will break your back." After it was lifted on to my back I would again carry it until I dropped it. We would do this until we carried it to where it had to be.

I remember one day it was snowing and very slippy underfoot, Mrs R asked us if we would fetch a quarter hundred weight of coal – this we did many times for her and usually were paid 6d (sixpence) – as we were carrying the coal back to her house there were not many men about so it took much longer than normal to get it to the house. The deal was we would get a 1/- (one shilling) that day for fetching the coal because of the bad weather. I feel at this point I must mention that neither Trevor or me had any wellies, gloves, overcoat or underwear on whenever we did any errands, we even had pumps on that had holes in the soles. The reason we always had holes in our pumps was because it was the only footwear we had, and when worn daily they wore out in a couple of weeks. Our clothes came from jumble sales and were always too small.

Any road up, when we did finally get back to the house, cold, wet and worn out the lady said, "Where on earth have you been? I've been waiting for this coal to light the fire for when my husband gets home from work, you have been messing about haven't you." No explanation would do, she just wouldn't believe a word I said. "It's the snow, Mrs R, it's slippy and there weren't any men around to lift it on to my back and there was a long queue." "You're lying to me, well I'm only giving you 2d each," she replied. Two pence, we were always polite, "Thank you, lady," I said whenever she asked me or Trevor to run errands for her, but after that we said, "no," but we said it very politely.

We were used by a lot of adults who didn't care about our welfare, we worked hard for them but they never appreciated what we did for them. One or two would say, "You are good lads for fetching these groceries for me, I can't pay you anything today, I will see you all right next time," but they never did, and we were too polite to remind them. Mrs R asked me and Trevor if we would go to the Gas Works to get a quarter of a hundred weight of coke, of course we said, "yes," even though we had said we would never run any more errands for her, so she gave us a 1/- (one shilling) that was for the bus fares (3d each way) and said she would give us 6d sixpence for getting the coke. I can't remember how much the coke was, I said, "Trevor, if we walk there and ride back we can save the bus fares." Halfway there it started to rain so we had to get on the bus because it was taking far too long to walk.

On arrival at the Gas Works there was a very long queue, so like everyone else we had to stand in line; the rain was very heavy and by this time we were soaked through to the skin. We paid at the office, got to where the coke came down a shoot, the man operating the shoot asked if I had another sack, "No, mister, I've only got this one it's OK." "Shame," he said, "I would have filled another one for you half price." "I wouldn't be able to carry it," I explained. His tone changed then, "Go on get out, there are other people waiting. Bloody kids," he said, to the next customer, "you wouldn't think parents would let kids out on days like this." As we struggled to get the sack on my back I heard him say to a man, "Have you got another sack?" so he asked everyone, he made his wages up that way I suppose.

I carried the sack of coke across the road to the bus stop, by this time the rain had soaked the coke through the sack which made a black slurry run down my back. As we waited at the bus stop the rain now was heavy, coke or coal wasn't allowed on buses, and when the bus arrived the conductor was upstairs so we got the coke onto the luggage rack – fortunately there were no pushchairs on there – and away we went. After a few minutes I looked round to make sure the bag of coke was still there, to my horror there was black slurry running from the sack off the luggage rack along the platform and off the bus. The conductor was going mad, "Who owns this bag of coal?" he was shouting as he ran up and down the stairs, "I will find out whose it is." The conductor hadn't noticed how wet and dirty we were, "Don't look round, don't say anything, Trev." "OK, Dave." "When we get near our stop, Trev, if the conductor goes upstairs I'm jumping off, we will have to carry it then, Dave." "I don't care, Trev, I'm jumping off, you stay on if you want to." "No, I'm with you, Dave."

The stop before ours a lady got off the bus, fortunately for us the conductor ran up the stairs still shouting, "Whose is this bag of coal?" This gave us the opportunity to jump off the bus without him seeing us, but as we stood up I noticed how wet and dirty the seat was. I was very worried thinking someone else would sit on that seat and ruin their clothes. As the bus started to move, I said, "Now, Trev," and with every ounce of strength left in me I grabbed the sack, threw it off the bus and jumped after it. The conductor was fuming, "I will remember you, look at the mess you have made on my bus." It was still raining hard, I got on my knees, got hold of the sack and with Trevor's help I stood up. The black slurry from the coke was running down my back and my legs and into my pumps, I was as black as the coke inside the sack, we were soaking, dripping wet.

Going to the Gas Works to get a bag of coke, getting very dirty and soaking wet, then to be told you are not getting paid makes it a day neither Trevor nor myself will ever forget.

When we got to the back door of the house, Mrs R opened the door and she was very angry, “You’ve been far too long, you’ve walked to save the bus fares haven’t you?” “No Mrs,” I said. “Look at the state of you, your mom won’t half give it to you when you get home, you are black and soaking wet.” “It’s the rain, Mrs.” “Don’t be cheeky to me, young man.” I never meant it the way she took it. “Well, I’m not paying you, here is a biscuit each.” It was a Rich Tea biscuit, stale and soft; she always gave us a biscuit and they were always stale. Upon that she closed the door. “Look, Trev, we are soaking wet, black, four hours’ work for a Rich Tea soft stale biscuit.” “Why does this keep happening to us, Dave?” “Dunno, Trev, it’s not fair all that work and no money.”

To cap it all a good hiding off my mom, bless her, she had to repair my clothes. Well it wasn’t the last time we worked and never got paid.

TRYING TO MAKE BOTH ENDS MEET

One of the things about Christmas that I loved, as well as getting presents on Christmas Day, was going into town with my mom and seeing all those lights, every shop decorated up, the long queues all round Lewis's out into the street. I only queued once with my mom to see Father Christmas at Lewis's, it took too long and all those people on those concrete stairs, to be honest it used to scare me. I always worried about stairs like that, nothing underneath them just sitting on the floor either end of the stairs. Going through the grotto was magical for children. I much preferred the Co-op Christmas grotto, it always seemed bigger and better to me and all those wonderful toys. I, like all children wanted them all.

I didn't go to see Father Christmas every year, I went up town with Mom every year but most times she had no money to spare. We always went round the Rag Market and the Meat Market, Mom was always looking for cheap presents for her children and cheap meat. I can still see and hear in my mind's eye. dealers holding toys up with outstretched arms shouting, "Only one left 6d, take this toy with this one then you can have the two for 9d – they are here to be sold." I used to think, I wish I had some money I would buy those. The man I loved to watch was Mr Lees, I assume he was the man selling the china with an overturned tea chest and a piece of carpet on top of it; he would bang the plates on it throw them up in the air and say, "These plates will last you a lifetime and they are strong," all the time banging them edgeways, by hitting them on the tea chests this way they wouldn't break and on the next stall shouting about the linen. Christmas is a Magical time.

One year I was in town with Mom at Christmas, she was really poor that year, she desperately tried to buy toys cheap. I can see her eyes now looking so anxious and watery asking, "Can you do those for 3d or 4d?" but no good, the dealers wouldn't drop the price. She was so worried, the pain she must have been going through just trying to get little presents for her children so we could wake up Christmas morning with something in our pillow case, yes always a pillow case. That year I remember seeing tears run down my mom's face and I asked, "Are you alright, Mom?" She said, "I've got something in my eye." I knew she was hurting, it's hurting with me writing it down. I had 8d in my pocket and offered it to my mom, "It's alright, son, buy yourself some sweets," she said. I went to a stall and saw a very pretty glass decorated with holly and bells; it was 6d so I bought it for my mom. "Here you are, Mom, I've bought you a present." She broke down and sobbed her heart out, with her arm round me she hugged me very tightly; she never said a word at that moment in time, her actions said it all. How can a child not remember such an occasion. As we walked out of the market she did say, "I love the glass you bought for me, but I can't buy you anything." "I don't want anything, Mom," I replied. I hurt her more than I could ever have imagined by trying to make her happy with a present; I shouldn't have done it should I, but as a child who loved his mom so much I thought a present would make her feel good.

When we got to the bus stop there was a very long queue, it seemed never ending; we waited for over an hour to get on the bus, the bus filled to capacity with people standing from the front of the bus right down to the platform. I hated being squashed and pushed around on those over-crowded buses. As the bus approached the next bus stop there was a very long queue because the bus had filled up from the terminus, it didn't stop the people standing there shouting and waving their fists. I was so relieved to get off that bus. Every year was the same, too many people, not enough buses in those days at Christmas time, a day in town meant a day.

RATION COUPONS

Stocktons local newsagent was on the corner of Trevor's Road, Swancote Road, and Mr Stockton ran that shop all through the war and well into the post-war years. One Sunday I was sent to that shop to buy a pound of sugar, it was against the law to sell groceries on a Sunday in those days, and when I asked for a pound of sugar a silence came over the shop. The lady looked around to see if any policemen were about, "There put it under your coat and don't let anyone see you with it," she said, all that in quite a worried voice. I was terrified, I put it under my jumper and ran like the wind, I felt like a criminal. It was a relief to walk into my house, my heart was going like a train, "Here you are, Mom, sugar, I'm not going on a Sunday again," I said. "OK, son," she said very calmly. I'm standing there still shaking.

The nicest memory I have of that shop was the day rationing finished, I was sitting in the house and was told I could go and buy some sweets without ration coupons. My mom gave me 3d (three pence), I ran to Stocktons and very nervously asked for 2oz of sherbet lemons. With shaking hands I handed over my 3d, she handed me the sweets and said, "There you are, bab." I got out of that shop very quickly; I will go and tell Trevor, I thought, I would excite him. "I know, I've been already with my mom, she bought me some," Trevor said.

One morning when rationing was still in force I was going through the sideboard looking for some string and pulled out what I thought was the drawer but I pulled the middle piece by mistake to find it was a secret drawer. I never knew it was there, Mom kept it a secret, I found Mom's ration book in there so I cut two sweet coupons out, ran up the road to find my mom, "Mom, Mom," I said, "I've found these," and handed the coupons over. "Sh," she said, "don't let anyone hear." She took me in the sweet shop and bought me 2oz of sweets.

I thought I had been very clever, I thought she will never know – children know nothing, do they – I had taken the last two coupons.

Next day I was playing with Trevor in the horse road, "David," Mom shouted, "I want you a minute." "Oh, Mom, I'm playing," I said. "Just for a minute," Mom said, so as I walked through the front gate she grabbed my arm and said, "You little bugga, you took those coupons out of my book that you gave me yesterday." "I found them, Mom," I said. "Oh you still want to lie to me, get the cane from the coal house," she angrily replied. She canned me three times for stealing the coupons and another three for lying to her. I never lied to her again. No tea that evening, it was five o'clock in the afternoon, and I was in bed with a very sore bottom.

RUN RABBIT RUN

Christmas, Carol singing night after night, I never got to that magic £1 mark, close 18/11, but never the one pound. Couple of my mates did, it's a magical time for children, Christmas Carols, coloured lights, Christmas trees, trimmings, how I loved those magical Christmases. Not coming from a family with lots of money it was make-do-and-mend season, a magical time for me but not so for my mother, the suffering she went through I can only imagine. My mate Johnny came down the road one Christmas Eve, he told me, "Your mom is up the shops crying her eyes out." He heard her say to a lady who wondered if she was alright, "I've got no money to buy my children any presents for Christmas," her heart and soul must have been torn in two. Just writing about it makes me feel tearful, that memory never fades. I actually remember what I got that Christmas, a colouring book with about eight pages in it and six crayons, no nuts or chocolate bar, we usually had these every Christmas but not that Christmas. I kept that book for a very long time. I've no idea why maybe because I felt there was so much hurt in my mom I kept it to say thank you. I loved it and it was very special to me, I don't really know. The pictures in were of Hopalong Cassidy (William Boyd).

The happy times of making paper chains, I remember the horrible taste after licking the gum to stick them together, crepe paper cut into strips and twisted, then they were pinned to the ceiling. Sometimes my sisters would sew cotton right through the middle of the crepe paper strips, then they would gather it up to make it looked fancy instead of flat twisted paper. There is one year I remember so well but not what year it was, I was very young. It's strange how certain things in your life stay as vivid memories like it was only yesterday. It was Christmas morning, well dinner time, I was lying on the floor in the living room as it was the warmest place in our house. I had a shooting game for my present – a little wire gun which when I squeezed the handle it released a spring that fired a round piece of wood at four animals, on a frame.

When hitting one of the animals, if you did, you scored points which was shown on the front of the game underneath each of the animals. My mother was putting the dinner out and shaking potatoes from the saucepan onto the plates on the table in the living room, lots of steam and mother saying, "You will have to move now, son, and play with that after dinner," just then Flanagan and Allen were singing on the wireless, "Run Rabbit Run." I loved that song and still do for it burned into my memory that very special Christmas morning and my wonderful mother, that memory will be mine to eternity. I love it. Thank you, Mr Flanagan and Allen.

One Christmas I was five years old, first year at school, I had a cowboy suit, it meant the world to me. On a Friday we were told we could bring a toy to school, "I will come in my cowboy outfit," I said. Another boy said he would come in his. I heard him telling another boy about his outfit, boy did it sound good. My mom saved 3d a week in a club to get my outfit. Any road up, I didn't go in it to school and I was glad I didn't as his outfit was all sheepskin, stones that looked like diamonds all round the hat, guns with pearl handles, diamond-studded cowboy boots with silver spurs attached – best outfit I've ever seen, even to this day. Mine was very basic, but it was mine. I did make-believe I had forgotten it, he was a spoiled child – what's that you say, sour grapes – you bet it was!

That same Christmas morning my sister Doreen had a doll, she went to walk down the stairs and dropped it, the doll smashed into a thousand pieces, did she sob. We only got one present, main present that is. Every Christmas me and Trevor went Carol singing, and with the money I got I bought my mom a tin tray and a pinny from a shop called Lathams. My Mom was a large lady, I never thought it wouldn't fit, the lady never asked me what size did I want. When Mom put it on I would say, "Oh, Mom, it's too small." She always said, "It's perfect, I love it." Bless her, buying for my mom always made me feel good.

As a seven year old I lay on the floor in the living room to play with my shooting game as it was the warmest place in our house. I remember that Christmas Day so well, because on the wireless Flanigan and Allan were singing 'Run Rabbit Run'.
I loved it, and still do, it made that Christmas morning stand out in my memory.

AUDLEY ROAD SECONDARY MODERN SCHOOL

Showing the infants playground where I played on my first day at school. The wooden building was divided into two classrooms; on the right was the infants at that time in 1948, on the left was the juniors. I was taught in both classrooms. That building has since been demolished.

AUDLEY ROAD SECONDARY SCHOOL

This is the juniors playground. The wooden buildings in the background are classrooms. The window facing was the Headmaster's office, Mr Taylor. The brick building on the right is an air raid shelter, and next to that was a wooden building that was the boys and girls toilets.

AUDLEY ROAD SECONDARY MODERN SCHOOL

The low brick buildings shown were air raid shelters built in the Second World War. Entrances were bricked up and they too have now been demolished. Me and my friends used to climb in them after school. They were at the far end of the juniors school playground. The grass is where we practised our football sometimes, but most times it was on the concrete playground. I played centre forward for the Juniors Football Team. Happy days!

JUGS OF BEER

The Glebe Pub had an outdoor, alas even that pub has now been demolished. This pub was my dad's second home, (more like his first). My mom, bless her, would have raised the Union Jack if she had seen the Glebe Pub being demolished, as this pub made a big contribution to me and all my family for the poverty we suffered. My dad drank there, any spare money and minute he had was spent there.

As I said, it had an outdoor, lots of children including me would earn money for fetching beer from this outdoor. I've taken beer bottles, jugs, pop bottles, once even a basin, usually for a pint of mild. They weren't supposed to serve beer to children but they always did. I was given 3d (three pence) by one lady and 4d (four pence) by another; never the men, only ever the ladies used to ask me to fetch beer.

Sometimes the men serving would be very grumpy and in a raised voice say, "Don't keep coming here for beer, I've enough to do," I used to think, why say don't come here for beer because that's what they sold. In the main barmaids were nice; only a couple of times I remember them saying, "I'm busy, you will have to wait," and wait we did for what seemed to be forever. Most times they would say, "I'm not supposed to sell you beer," but they always did.

PIG SWILL

A friend of mine whose name was Douglas, he lived at the bottom of the adjoining road to my road, his Dad kept pigs in their back garden, they did this all through the war because of food shortage. I loved to watch the pigs being fed, when the food was being poured into the trough the pigs went wild, like they had never been fed, they pushed each other violently. It fascinated me so much I offered to go round the houses with Douglas and collect the pig swill, it was a smelly job but I just loved doing it.

Dougie lived across the road from Billy, two doors away from John, Eddy lived across the road from John, Trevor lived six doors away from Eddy and I lived over the road from Trevor. Six of us, we spent many a year together, we went everywhere together, at one stage we all rummaged on the tip. As we entered our teens we sort of split in half, not completely for we sometimes all got together and went cycling, swimming, football. Me and Trevor were like brothers, we spent every day together, well almost, Johnny sort of mixed with all of us, out with them one day and us another.

About once a fortnight I would help Douglas collect the pig swill, so did Trevor; the pig swill was in dustbins usually at the side of the houses, we could only go to certain houses because there was another family that kept pigs a few doors away from Trevor's house, so they never touched Dougie's pig bins and he never touched their pig bin. As we were colleting one day Dougie looked really worried, "What's the matter, Dougie?" I asked. "There isn't enough swill for the pigs," his bin round was done in two halves, one set of houses one fortnight and the other half the following fortnight. In those days people didn't waste much food, well it wasn't long after the Second World War and rationing was still on, and times were still very hard for the working classes so pig keeping was even more difficult. "Well, Dougie, let's take one or two and half empty them from the other pig keepers' bins."

"We can't, Dave, we have an agreement, we don't touch the theirs and they don't touch ours." "Well, if we don't empty the bins, only take a bit out of each bin." "That should be all right, Dave," so that's what we did. When we got back to his house he said, "I haven't any firewood to boil the swill up," so I climbed over the fence to the field at the back of his garden to find some wood. Dougie said, "I've looked all over that field, Dave, there isn't any."

I looked and found a small handful in the field, wood was very hard to find in those days, everyone used wood to light their coal fires, so with the few sticks I found and with what Dougie had, he lit the fire under the pig swill. As the wood started to burn Dougie began to throw the bread on to keep the fire going, I never knew bread would burn like it did. "I hate burning the bread, Dave, but it's the only way I can get the swill to boil." All sorts went into that swill and to think how they go on today about hygiene, health and safety, it has to make you smile, I never caught anything, but I never liked the smell of those bins.

As I was walking back to my house the other family who kept pigs, their two sons were walking towards me, they shouted, "You've been taking our pig swill." "We have not," I said. "Yes you have, you were seen and they told us it was you." "Well it wasn't me," I kept insisting. "We will have the same amount back out of your bins next week, we have to feed our pigs as well you know," they shouted back.

My mom kept the swill for that family but it was more than my life was worth to take my mom's. I was more afraid of my mom more than any boy. Every Christmas the people who saved the swill all year were given a nice piece of pork to say thank you. The man who kept the pigs went to see Dougie's dad about us taking his swill. Dougie got a good hiding and I was banned from going round to see the pigs; it seemed that it was set in stone never to touch the other family's pig swill.

Enjoying watching the pigs while waiting for the pig swill to come to the boil. It was very interesting to see the pigs fight to get the best position when I poured the swill into the trough. After watching the pigs feed I now know why my mom used to say to me at meal times you are like a pig in a trough.

MY TALKING BOOTS

It was a Saturday morning, I ran some errands for two neighbours and I had earned 9d (nine pence). Trevor was going with his mom to the Birmingham Rag Market. The Atlas Cinema had its normal Saturday matinee at 12 noon, we always referred to it as the flicks, so of I went to the flicks. I walked down Audley Road, I completely forgot about my right boot, the toe cap was flapping just like it was talking or singing, it was hanging on by a thin piece of leather; on the left-hand side there was a long piece of leather hanging where the toe cap had been ripped off. I was able to tuck that piece of leather inside my boot which made the boot look normal and the toe cap OK. Every time I did it I used to think, that's better, so off to the flicks I go.

They were showing Hopalong Cassidy – I loved that cowboy with his black clothes and his silver accessories. At the end of the film we were like a herd of cattle all rushing to get to the bus stop first. I would normally walk home, but I must have been feeling lazy that afternoon. I had 2d (two pence) left, it was only two stops so I waited for the bus, and while I was standing there a boy standing next to me gave me a nudge with his elbow. I turned to see what he wanted, with a snigger and a sneer he said, "Your toe cap is flapping." I felt embarrassed and ashamed, I had completely forgotten about my boot. "Why don't you get a pair of boots like mine," he was sniggering all the time he was saying it, "mine are polished, why don't you polish yours?" "My mom can't afford any at the moment, I'm getting some new ones next week," I told him, I wasn't but I didn't know what else to say to him.

By this time there were lots of boys and girls waiting for the bus and they were all looking and laughing, I was praying for the bus to turn up, I even thought of running from the bus stop to get away from the humiliation I was suffering. Just as I was about to run, the bus turned up, I was so relieved, I went upstairs on the bus (I always went up stairs) and hid my feet under my seat so my boots were not seen. When I got off the bus I must admit I was close to tears but I held them back. Where I came from boys were tough and never cried, at least not if anyone could see you, I grew up to believe that.

As I walked into our kitchen my mom could see I was upset, "What on earth's the matter, David?" she asked, "Nothing, Mom," I replied. "Yes there is, now what's up?" a mother knows her children well. I told her how the boy had laughed at me because my toe cap on my boot was flapping and all the boys and girls at the bus stop were also laughing. She hugged me and said, "You are better than all them, you would never take the rise out of anyone would you, son, that was in the same boat as you." "Never, Mom," I said (taking the rise meant taking the mick). I was taught to help people never to belittle anyone; if I did, which I never did, Mom would have belted me till I couldn't sit down, she was a stickler for good manners and respect. "I will ask your father when he comes home from work if he has any money to help me get you a pair of pumps."

I felt very happy at that moment, all I wanted was to look normal just like all the other children. I got my new pumps the next day, I felt really good walking around with footwear that looked OK. My thoughts were at that time, no one can take the rise out of me now. It's not good for children to feel this way, is it? But ay, that's life because when those pumps got holes in the soles which was not long, I was back to putting cardboard in them and tucking my socks under my feet. Life can be so cruel and hard, even for children. For mothers even harder.

Wish I had some new boots so people wouldn't laugh.

FAGGOTS AND PEAS

Carmichaels was what everyone where I lived called "the faggots and pea shop". Really it was a cooked meats shop – ham, cooked pork, cheese, cereals, biscuits – all those sorts of items, but the Carmichaels we knew were famous for their faggots and peas. People would queue for nearly an hour before they opened to buy their famous faggots. There's been as many as fifty people waiting, if you were at the front of the queue you got plenty of gravy, at the back of the queue and you would definitely get no gravy; in fact many a time you got no faggots because they were sold out, so many a time I was sent to get in the queue early.

I would listen to people talking, their daughters having babies and what a bad time they had, talking about someone dying, women's troubles – I heard just about every disease known to man, ha, ha in this case women. We stood outside winter and summer it was a sight to see some of the people – men and women dressed to kill, some in slippers and aprons – well you can imagine, and scruffy little me always needing a wash; and to see the different utensils they were holding that always fascinated me – jugs, kettles, saucepans, big mugs.

Some people went to the hardware shop known as Suches, which was a couple of doors away to buy a basin or bowl which was always dusty and on occasions the shopkeeper would be asked to wash out the bowl which they kindly did with a smile. This shop did quite a trade because of the faggot and pea shop. I tell you what, I'm proud to have been a part of it, it's my history – those faggots and peas are the best I have ever tasted, yes I've tried the Black Country ones a few times, not to my liking. Carmichaels have never been equalled in my humble opinion.

The one time I went to get some faggots for my mom I was at the back of the queue; I was supposed to get four faggots but because I messed about and was late, I only got three – the last three I might add, and no gravy. It was raining so I got water in with them, well it looked like gravy, only see-through. Well I got a clip round the ear and no faggots. These faggots were their own recipe, many people my mom told me asked for that recipe but they always said no. They had a daughter the same age as me, I wonder did she have that famous recipe?

ALL GROWN UP

The first time I ever had long grey trousers it was in February; there was snow on the ground and it was very cold. When I went to school everyone noticed this scruffy boy had a new pair of trousers, they took the mick for the first morning and then it all faded. Well they were really warm after wearing short trousers.

After school had finished and after I had my tea I went with my two friends to Manor Park playing fields where there was quite a slope at the end of the football pitches. We had an old tin tray that we used for sledging down the slope, and lots of children were there sledging – what we called the posh kids as they had real sledges, not a tin one like we did. We had every bit of fun as they did. All we had was a piece of tin for a sledge. We were jealous of them if I'm honest, I always wanted a proper sledge but never got one. I never found one on the rubbish tip. I bet those posh kids never had the freedom of childhood that I had.

On the way home I looked down and saw a tear in my nice new trousers. One day and I had ruined a new pair of trousers – well, there was another good hiding coming my way. Not only ripped but dirty as well. It's no wonder I was called "Scruff".

SIXPENCE FOR SWEETS

To go to the cinema in the 1940s and the 1950s was a real treat. Trevor and I used to stand outside the cinema, sometimes until it was quite late, to go in as the second picture had just started. Children were never allowed to go in alone if the picture had an "A" certificate. There were three types of certificate films – for children to watch without an adult it was a "U" certificate and when it was an "A" a child always had to be accompanied by an adult. If it was an "X" certificate children were not allowed in at all. So it was "A", "U", "X". I think it has all changed now.

Sometimes I would stand there alone but most of the time Trevor was with me and we would ask anyone to take us in – courting couples, old dears, people with children. Thinking about it, it was rare to see mom, dad and children. To older people I would say "take us in, Mister," or "take us in, Lady," hold out my hand with the sixpence in it. If we had to have an adult to take us in because the film was an "A" we used to get a lot of comments, most I can't repeat; the most common one was of course "No", usually quite loud, when some kind couple said "Yes" I gave them my sixpence. Most times I was told to stand at the back of them or past the kiosk so as not to be seen with them. I must have looked a sight. Only once do I remember a couple allowing me to sit by them. I was told to keep quiet, don't fidget, sit still. I sat there frightened to death to move, well as you know children always fidget.

One evening I was standing there on my own asking, "take me in Lady," when a pretty young lady with very dark shoulder-length hair with a three-quarter length coat on and a scarf round her neck said, "Of course I will, Bab." I handed her my sixpence and to my surprise she said, "It's alright, Bab, I will pay for you, you go and buy some sweets for yourself." I said, "Is it alright if I sit by you?" "Of course you can," she replied. That never happened before and it never happened again. God bless that kind lady.

You see if you were sitting by yourself and there wasn't an adult either side of you and the picture was an "A" certificate the usherette knew someone had taken you in, she would shine her torch on you and throw you out. When couples did take you in you were told, "We will take you in but you ain't sitting by us." Even now that thought makes me feel very uncomfortable but of course I was very scruffy so I suppose I can't blame them. I remember the courting couples – the lady's hair was always nice and always looked like they were going to a wedding and she always had bright red lipstick on; and the man had a smart suit and Brylcreemed hair, polished shoes and a smart tie, her on his arm and always looked very happy and very much in love. Would you want a scruffy little kid sitting by you when you were in love? Neither would I. (Well I'm not sure, I was that scruffy kid.)

Oh yes, the next day I told Trevor, "A lady took me in and paid for me and I bought sweets with the sixpence." He was so jealous every time we stood outside the Atlas Cinema, Stechford, and was asking to be taken in, he would say, "Is this the lady that paid for you to be taken in?" He was hoping if we saw her she would pay for us again, secretly so was I also, alas I never saw her again.

It's wonderful remembering the past, even though it was hard but the small things we achieved made us very happy, as they do now.

PLAYING WITH FIRE

As children in those days we all played together in the horse road, as my mom always called it. The girls played alongside of the boys, and I very much liked to watch the girls skipping they were so fast and nimble. I tried a few times to join them but my feet were not fast enough, and it wasn't long before they told me to clear off because I was spoiling their game. I was quite good at hopscotch, though never good enough to beat the girls.

I had such wonderful times, those were wonderful years for all us children, we were poor, not well-clothed but when playing in the horse road with all my friends nothing else mattered; we were all good neighbours to one another and that combination can never be beaten. I don't care how rich or poor anyone is, with good friends and neighbours like I had you were opulent.

One day when we were playing in the road I had a box of matches; I'm not sure why I had matches, I think I got them from my mom's kitchen because one of our the girls had one of those fire cans we used to swing round. Anyway, I lit the paper in the can (I think it was Nanette, Trevor's sister that was playing with the fire can), she swung it round till it got red hot and glowed. Some of the girls were as tough as the boys; one girl named Ann said to me, "You shouldn't play with fire, nor should you have matches." I remember I lit a match, I thought I would play her up and singe her hair, boy did I get scared, I never knew hair burned the way it did, her hair went up in flames. Ann's sister Rita rushed over to her and put out the flames. I can't remember what Ann said to me, we all carried on playing after I apologized to her, I remember that day well.

I still see Ann and her sister Rita from time to time, Rita like me loves talking about the past. Ann was playing one day with my sister Janet when June a girl who came out to play (she lived two doors away from Ann) had a blue ribbon in her hair. Ann said, "That's my ribbon she has in her hair, I lost it the other day." So

Ann said to June (who now lives in America), “That’s my ribbon you’ve got in your hair, June.” She said, “No it is not, my mom bought it for me last week.” (I don’t think Ann for one minute thought maybe she could be wrong.) “Yes it is,” Ann replied, “I’ve got the other ribbon in the house that matches that one, I will go and get it,” and she ran down to the back of her house but when she was halfway there she tripped (I can still hear her screams to this day). She ripped open her top lip and damaged her two front teeth; her top lip is scarred but she is still a nice looking lady.

All my friends that I grew up with are down-to-earth lovely people, it’s wonderful to keep in touch with old friends and reminisce, it makes one appreciate old times.

DAD'S WORKS

Most of the factories when I was a boy had Christmas parties for the children of their work force. It was great fun, as young children we loved it, it was very special to us to get jelly and blancmange, fruit, even cake. The icing on the cake, as the saying goes, was a present to take home after the party had ended.

My dad worked at the Metropolitan Camel and Carriage Works, they made trains. The factory was at the Gate, Saltley, Birmingham, I went there three times, my dad worked there all through the war. The present was sometimes a gun or a game, one year I got a gun, another year I got a Snakes and Ladders game, the third year I got a book and a compendium of games.

My dad used to put on a show for all the children with my eldest brother, they always did the same play about school boys, they were very good. My dad left that firm for a short while and started to work for a firm called S U Carbareter. At the train works he was a radial driller, at his new company he was a labourer; why he left the train company I have no idea, yet he spent many years with the train company.

Anyway I went twice to the Christmas parties at his new firm, I was given a colouring book both times as a present. He left that firm after about eighteen months and returned to his old firm the Metropolitan Camel And Wagon Works, his boss was my mom's brother, my uncle Bob. At one Christmas party my sister Doreen got her present – dolls furniture – she wasn't happy with it, she thought she was too old for it, so she got in the queue again. The man said, "You've been round before haven't you?" "No," she replied, so he gave her another present – did she moan, another set of dolls house furniture! Some girls had dolls, some had games, my sister wanted a game. That was the last Christmas party I ever went to at that firm, that year I got a red gun.

My dad was a member of the British Legion, I went there a couple of times to their Christmas parties. The first time was after Christmas, they always had their Christmas parties after Christmas, we were taken to the Aston Hippodrome to see *Puss in Boots*, it was a wonderful show. The British Legion was at the back of my house, and I got the coach outside the legion. We were given a bag with sweets, an apple and an orange in it, we got out of the coach and rushed in like a herd of cattle to get to what we thought would be the best seats in the hippodrome, boy we were noisy that afternoon! The apple was sour, I ate mine because I didn't get fruit very often. The boy sitting next to me threw his apple, it hit a man on the back of his head, it really hurt him, he was very angry, he was looking around hoping to see who had thrown it. I was thinking, I wish he had given me that apple. When the curtains went back it went very quiet, I was in heaven, that was the first and last time I went to a pantomime, I shall remember the song they sang till the day I die, THIS IS THE HOUR FOR US TO SAY GOOD NIGHT. I was very moved by it, the colours, the atmosphere, it truly was electric, while writing this I find I want to go again.

FIRE CANS

Fire cans – I loved playing with these! I realise now of course just how dangerous they were for young children to play with. If when on the tip we found a treacle tin, we would find a nail and with a stone we would punch holes in it, we then looked for a piece of wire and tied it to the sides of the tin, put paper and wood in it. I lit the paper, then swing the can round till the wood was well and truly lit and keep putting wood in until the can glowed red hot. If at home we sorted over the slack in the coal house, coal made the can glow red really quickly.

My sister Doreen was swinging a can in our front garden one afternoon, "Dave," she shouted, "come here and pick this piece of wood up for me." "Can I have a go then?" I asked. "If you go into the coal house and sort through the slack for some lumps of coal," she answered. "If I do, then can I have a go?" I pleaded. "Yes OK, but only if you find a lot," she replied. So into the coal house I went and came out looking blacker than the coal, with the whitewash off the walls all down my back. Doreen was very pleased with the amount that I had found, after putting it in the can and getting it very hot after she swung it round a few times I said, "Can I have a go now?" Doreen again asked me to pick the wood up, and I bent down to pick up the wood as she was swinging the glowing red hot can round and it hit me over my left eye and split it wide open – off to the hospital with Mother to have it stitched. On returning home Doreen was given a good hiding and fire cans were banned, never to be seen again, not anywhere near our house anyway. (I loved to hear the swishing sound as the cans were swung round!)

Making our fire cans glow in the dark.

HEADING HOUSE BRICKS

There is an alleyway at the rear of the shops in Glebe Farm, the alleyway is the delivery access to the shops backing onto it, air raid shelters were on one side, with Audley Road School backing onto them. The shelters were for the infants and juniors to use during an air raid. I went to this school at the age of five to the tender age of fifteen, when I left in 1958 I thought I was all grown up.

One morning walking to the shops with Trevor, we noticed a builder's lorry parked in the alley, a builder was working on the walls surrounding the backyards of the shops. We could hear all the banging, rubble being thrown onto the back of the lorry, quick as a flash as the saying goes I said, "Come on, Trev, we might be able to earn some money." Climbing over the rubble without any thought of danger I said to the builder, "Excuse me, Mister, do you want any help?" "Yes, lads, would you start to throw all the bricks onto the back of the lorry?" "Yes, easy," I said. "Good, you start there," he said, pointing to the entrance of the yard. "Nice and steady," I said to Trevor, "if we make it last we might be able to come tomorrow and earn more money." We worked really well together and before long we had cleared the whole entrance.

All was going well when our friend Johnny shouted, "Hey, what's going on? How did you get this job?" "We asked if he needed any help and he said yes," I answered. "How much is he paying you?" asked John, "He never said," I replied. "I'm going to ask him," John said.

The builder said, "You three get in a line and I will throw the bricks to you, then you," he said pointing at Trevor, "can throw them onto the lorry."

All was going well, we must have moved seven or eight hundred bricks, the ends of our fingers were very sore by this time. I threw a brick to Trevor but because his fingers were sore he dropped it and I didn't turn to look at Johnny. The chain had broken down, by this time Trevor had dropped the brick but it was too late, as I turned back to tell Johnny to hold it, a brick that he had thrown flew and hit me on the head. The blood cascaded down my face, the builder came rushing over, I put my finger over the cut, "I'm alright," I shouted, "don't touch me," as I couldn't stand people messing with me when I had been hurt (I'm still the same now).

"I think I can manage on my own now, lads," the builder said, "thanks for your help," and not a penny did we receive, we had worked for nothing. When I stopped bleeding, we all started playing football in the street. I never cleaned that cut, I had a beautiful big lump the next morning and it was very sore for a week afterwards.

THE QUEEN

One Bonfire Day, well a week before really, me and Trevor were around Castle Bromwich looking for firewood for our bonfire. Well, we found these two big branches which were quite heavy, we were dragging them past Bradford Hall which we all thought was haunted. Facing the Hall are two rows of what I think are Chestnut trees, I think the owner of the hall had these trees planted so when he looked out of his window he looked down the avenue of trees.

Anyway, me and Trevor were pulling those branches along this avenue of trees, we came to the main Chester Road, you can imagine how dirty and scruffy we were, nearly by the Chester Road, I couldn't believe my eyes, the Queen was passing! Well she laughed as I waved and shouted, "Hi, Queen," we were very close to her. Wonder what she thought when she saw two dirty scruffy kids from Birmingham pulling two big tree branches behind them. I will never forget seeing the Queen laugh at me and Trevor.

I bet if the authorities had known we were there looking like that we would have been hidden away or cleaned up. That's my claim to fame, and at least it gave the Queen a laugh. I think that was the day she opened All Saints Church at Shard End. That's the church I was married at because my girlfriend lived at Shard End and you had to get married in the parish where your intended came from and that was Shard End.

Author and Trevor waving to the Queen. As she passed, her head went back as she laughed and when she saw two dirty little urchins dragging branches for their bonfire. She was on her way to open All Saints Church in Shard End, Birmingham, in the 1950s.

Bradford Hall is the building in the background. Trevor and I were dragging branches one bonfire night, and as we approached the Chester Road we saw the Queen.

This picture is showing the Chester Road where we saw the Queen.

A PENNY FOR HIM

At the start of November I called for my friend Trevor and said, "Hey, Trev, I have had a great idea." "Oh yeah? What have I got to do now?" "Well, Trev, I thought if I dress you as Guy Fawkes and sit you in a pushchair I can push you to the bus stop up the road, at the shops you can hold a cup in your hand and I will stand at the side of you and ask for a penny for the guy. Can you get a pair of your dad's old trousers?" "I can get my dad's old overcoat and his flat cap." "If we go round to the back of corn shop" (this shop was called Turners) "there is usually a lot of straw on the floor by their back gate – we could go and pick it up and use it to put in your trouser legs, your coat, out the sleeves and out of the cap; then we need to find some string to tie round the bottom of the trousers to hold the straw in and round the sleeves and we can put the straw under your hat." "OK," said Trevor, "Let's do it." So I dressed him up and stood outside the bus stop with him holding his cup for the pennies. We didn't do very well only 7d. So I had a bright idea – I started to push him all around the houses and I knocked on lots of doors and asked for a penny for the guy.

We got lots of different comments! Some would have a good laugh and give us 2d. Some would tell us to clear off and the main comment was, "Sod off, you bloody little scroungers." We always used the money we got to go swimming or to go to the pictures (the cinema) and of course we would buy sweets – my favourites sweets at that time were sherbet lemons, they had sherbet in the middle of them.

We also used the money that we collected to go roller skating. Trevor's brother Tony always came with us. We had great fun, there were lots of rough boys that went to this roller rink. I think they had about three bouncers, I saw many a lad thrown out of there and I mean thrown. I mostly stayed in the middle of the rink that's where all us wimps went. Yes I was a wimp! I was knocked flying more than once especially when there was six or more of them holding hands. The one on the end would be flipped round at such a speed it was very dangerous. I was sent flying a couple of times by the one on the end of the line, he couldn't stop. I even saw them hit the barrier and get knocked out because of the speed they were travelling and some got really bad cuts. They only did this when they thought the bouncer wasn't around because it wasn't allowed. It was soon stopped as soon as the bouncers had seen it start. Everyone that was in the line would get thrown out. They always knew that they would get thrown out as soon as they started.

One afternoon, when Tony Trevor and I had earned enough money from Guy Fawking, we went to the skating rink. When they gave me my pair of skates the lace was half missing in the one skate. I took it back to complain but even the ladies behind the counter were as rough as the bouncers and I was told to clear off and make do. At the end of the session some lads would not hand their skates back in and leave them lying around because they had sneaked out of the side doors. So I decided to take a lace from one of boots and put it in my boot, when a bouncer came up to me, grabbed hold of me by the scruff of the neck and accused me of trying to steel the skates. He was shaking me violently and threatening to get the police. Bearing in mind I was only a young whippersnapper at the tender age of about nine, I was almost in tears as I tried to explain that I was only replacing the lace because the one that I had been given was not long enough. I had asked the lady at the counter and she refused to change the boots, so he frog-marched me to the counter to confirm what I was saying was the truth. After the lady had confirmed what I was saying was the truth the bouncer said, "Sorry, son, but we do lose a lot of skates from people stealing them." I said, "I love coming here, Mister, I love to skate." Then in a very stern voice he said, "Do not ever do it again, I shall remember you and if I find you in here and you are taking laces out of the skates even if you have paid I will still throw you out and you will not get a refund!"

Trevor and I loved doing the things none of our friends would do, and me dressing Trevor up as Guy Fawkes was I think one of them. We had fun, Trevor and I.

This roller rink was off the Golden Hillock Road Small Heath, it was actually in Wharf Road I think. We went to this roller rink many, many times and we always walked from Glebe Farm, Stechford, which was one hell of a walk. It must have been a good ten miles which was a long way for young lads. Later on it was turned into a bingo hall. When I worked for Coca Cola, I delivered to that rink, and as I looked round that old building I had such a lot of memories come back to me. I believe it has now been demolished. It was a lovely old building, it was made of timber.

When I think back about those days roller skating I remember how that bouncer terrified me. Mind you it was an exciting time for a young lad.

BLOOD, SWEAT AND TEARS

Trevor and I sat on my garden wall, we would put our brains together (which were very few – neither of us could read or write very well) to find a way of making money. We had some, what I now know as hairbrained ideas – digging out a drive was most definitely one of them.

We went to our local community centre to ask if they needed any jobs doing. In the building was a man who worked for the government, he looked after children who had been naughty and got into trouble. He was called a Probation Officer, I had no idea at that time what that was or who he was at that time. I was off school getting over a cold, I can't remember why Trevor was off school. We knocked on the door a man opened the door of the community centre, "Do you want any jobs doing, Mister?" I asked. The first thing he said was, "Why are you not at school?" "We are getting over a cold," I explained to him. "Oh I see," he said. As I turned to walk away after he had told us he didn't require any jobs doing, I spotted through a half opened door at the end of the corridor a snooker table so I asked if we could play on it, "Yes you can," he said, to my great surprise, "so long as you are very quiet." "Thank you, Mister," we both said together.

About just over an hour had passed when the man came into the room where we were. "I say, you boys, are you interested in gardening?" Without a second's thought I said, "Yes we like gardening we do it all the time." We knew absolutely nothing about gardening, my mind was in overdrive wondering how much money we could make. "I live in Castle Bromwich, do you know where that is?" he asked. Well of course we didn't know. I replied, "We will find it, Mister, if you give us directions." "Tell you what, boys, I will leave early tonight and take you in my car and show you the way – is that all right, boys?" "Yes, Mister," Trevor said very quickly. "OK, boys, you carry on playing snooker."

“Wow, Trev, a ride in a car!” we were excited I can tell you. We got into his car, it smelt of leather; I can still smell that to this very day, it was an Austin. “Boys, you will have to walk back, it’s not that far only I have to go out as soon as I’ve shown you the job.” “That’s OK, Mister, we like walking don’t we, Trev?” “Yeah,” we would say anything to earn money plus to get a ride in a car, we didn’t know anyone with a car. I was ten, Trevor was eleven, we thought he was a millionaire because he had a car. As we were going along the road I was hoping to see one of our friends so we could wave to them – they would have been ever so jealous but we never passed one of them.

We arrived at his house and he parked the car on the road. “Here you are, boys, this is what I want you to do: I want this Hawthorne hedge taking down and this sandstone wall. I have a wheelbarrow you can use to take the stones round the back right to the bottom of the garden, the Hawthorne hedge you can drag round the back. When you have done that I want the soil digging out and again barrowing round the back to the bottom of the garden but keep all the items separate so it will be easy for me to move at a later date. The reason for doing this, boys, I want to put my car on my garden to keep it off the road – think you can manage that boys?” he asked. Me and Trevor stood by the wall with the hedge on top of it, it must have been twelve foot or more high and for a ten and an eleven year old this was a mammoth task. “Can you start tomorrow, boys? I want it done as quick as possible.” “Yes, Mister,” I replied.

Next morning we walked from our houses which was in Glebe Farm, Stechford, to Castle Bromwich. It was a nice warm day nice for a walk; it took us thirty-five minutes to walk there, and as we walked up the path the lady of the house came out to us, “There you are, boys, I’ve put out the tools ready for you, mind you clean them when you have finished with them – there is a spade, a saw and a pair of secateurs.” (What are those, I thought to myself, I’ve never heard of them.) “And here is a lump hammer,” she explained, “it’s for knocking the wall down, and the barrow is round the back when you need it." I asked for a drink of water before we started hoping she would give us pop, we got what I asked for – water.

We started to cut down the Hawthorne hedge, we didn't know it had thorns! We got injected, scratched, both of us had ripped our arms to bits and it took us all day to dig up and cut up that hedge. I was by this time very tired, so was Trevor. We stopped work at 4.30 p.m., I remember that because the lady came out with a glass of home-made Ginger Beer and a fairy cake each, best Ginger Beer I've ever tasted – that might be because I was tired, hot and very dry and very hungry. We only had two glasses of Ginger Beer and two fairy cakes all day. The lady next door asked the time, that's how I remember it was 4.30 p.m. We had left most of the hedge lying on the front garden ready to put round the back next morning.

We arrived home worn out. "Trev, it's harder than I thought it would be." "It is, Dave, ain't it. Shall we not go tomorrow?" "Let's see how we feel in the morning," I said. Next morning feeling good after a good night's sleep I called for Trevor, and like me feeling refreshed after a night's sleep he said, "Right, Dave, let's go, we won't let it beat us will we?" "No way, Trev." We worked in the only set of clothes we possessed, our seven-days-a-week suit HA HA! We were not very clean, our clothes that is.

On arriving we took what was left of the hedge round to the back garden, it must have been 80 yards long, then we started to take down the sandstone wall. This took us three days, I was pushing the wheelbarrow, I grew tired very quick pushing the barrow with big stones in it, I ended up putting one stone at a time in. Trevor and I found this work to be too much for us both at times. After the hedge and wall were down we started to dig out the soil, which we found to be the hardest job to date – many, many barrow loads – we took just over a week to complete the job, without a doubt it was far too big a job for two little urchins like us. Our clothes were more ruined than they were before.

We cleaned up, put all the tools away, "Cor, Trev, I wonder how much he will pay us?" Out came the lady with two glasses of Ginger Beer and two fairy cakes. "Well done, boys, my husband will be pleased, you have worked very hard. He'll be home soon, I've phoned him to tell him you have finished the drive."

We had great expectations, saying to each other 10/- (ten shillings) each, well at least 8/- (eight shillings). We were sitting on the wall the other side of the garden when Trevor said, "Here he is, Dave." He drove his car on to his drive for the first time, got out of the car, hands on hips looking up and down his new drive saying, "Wonderful, wonderful, boys, thank you very much you have worked really hard you should be very proud of yourselves," he said, "thank you very much," shook our hands walked into the house and closed the door. I looked at Trevor, we were both in shock. "He will come out in a minute and pay us, Dave." "Yeah of course he will." Wrong, he never showed his face; we waited a good fifteen minutes – all that work for glasses of Ginger Beer and fairy cakes. "In future, Trev, I'm going to ask how much they will pay before we start work." "Yeah we will too, Dave."

Every time I pass that house in my car, whoever is with me I say, "Me and Trevor dug that drive out." "We know, you have told us before," they always replied. My wife said, "Dave, why don't you write it down and put it in book form," so I have, that's how come you are reading it.

This is the drive that Trevor and I dug out
in the Castle Bromwich area of Birmingham.

BIRMINGHAM HIPPODROME

Trevor's brother Tony and I went to the Atlas Cinema; again I have no idea why Trevor wasn't with us as the three of us went everywhere together. Whenever we went swimming it was the three of us which was quite often. Any road up, while I was watching the film Tony suddenly said, "Dave, look what I've just found – a wage packet." When he opened it there to his amazement was £2.10/- (two pounds ten shillings) inside of it. TONY GAVE ME THE TEN SHILLING NOTE. Boy, did I feel rich!

We left the cinema and got the bus to Birmingham city centre, and walked round the town for a while Tony said, "Ay Dave, have you ever been to the Hippodrome?" "Cor no," I replied. "OK, come on then you are in for a treat." So in we go, it was the first showing of the day; David Hughes a singer appeared. I was waving to him and Tony looked at me, laughed and said, "Why are you waving to a man?" I felt such a fool! After the singer, Morecambe and Wise came on – I liked them, and when the show had finished I got David Hughes' autograph. That was the first time I had heard of him; it was also the first time I had heard of Morecambe and Wise

When I got married I gave my autograph book to my wife's two little brothers but they ripped it up – thing was, it contained all my school friends' wishes to me and their signatures on the day I left school. I really miss that book, that's one of the reasons I'm putting down all my memories in book form. I can then at least read through it to give my memory a nudge as the years pass and my memory fades.

THE COAL MERCHANTS

One warm summer's day, around nine o'clock in the morning, I walked to the tip as I usually did looking for old shoes for my mom to burn on the fire to keep us warm. I know it was summer but the summer evenings were sometimes chilly; any road up, the old shoes were saved for these chilly nights. The reason we had no coal was because my mom would pay weekly for the coal but she fell behind with the payments so the coal merchants would not let her have any more coal until the bill was paid in full. It was a treat when finally I watched with much interest the coalman carrying a hundred weight of coal through the kitchen to what my mom called the "coal ole" (a cupboard under the stairs).

One thing has always stuck in my mind and it always used to puzzle me as a young lad of early years, my mom (never my dad) used to whitewash the coal ole walls. I was always sent to the hardware shop in Glebe Farm, Stechford, which was called Suches. I used to ask for a ball of white and a washing blue. The ball of white would be broken up in a bucket then filled up with cold water, then the blue would be added. The boiler stick that my mom used for getting clothes out of the boiler after being washed would be used for stirring, what I now know was chalk, until all was dissolved. (This stick was also used a few times on my backside when I played up.) Then with a large brush it would be brushed onto the three walls, very wet and messy I seem to remember.

As I said, what puzzled me when the coalman went to tip the coal from the bag that was on his back, my mom would say, "I've whitewashed the walls, don't dirty them." The poor coalman would try so hard to keep the coal from hitting the walls, as if his job wasn't hard enough, but he did what he was told and said, "I haven't dirtied your walls, Mrs Prosser." He knew my mom, he only lived a few doors away from our house. A thought just came to me, every time I went to get some coal from the coal ole the white would come off the walls and made a real mess of my clothes, so sometimes when the coal was low it was a real struggle to get the coal without getting the whitewash on my clothes.

The house the coalman lived in was number 38 (the same number as our house), his road was just round the corner from our house. I remember Mom talking one day to my dad and saying that we should have had that house the coalman lived in and there was a mix-up at the council office because both houses had the same number. There had been a mix-up with the keys and she asked the coalman at the time to swap houses but he wouldn't swap, he said he was happy with his house. My mom always said she preferred the coalman's house – was this because she thought the grass was greener on the other side as the saying goes? I think our house, which was a semi-detached on a corner, was far better than the coalman's house which was a terraced house with an entry for access to the back garden; at least we had our own back gate giving us access without having to go through the front door. Mind you, the coalman's house had a back gate but they had to share an entry.

2/- TO SPEND

I found as I was growing up girls were the most cruel creatures on God's green earth. I suppose when one is poorly dressed, even scruffy looking, it would make girls not want to be near you or touch you. It started in the infants when we had dancing lessons – all the girls would say, "I'm not dancing with you." I usually was left out on my own, you would have thought the teacher would have noticed this and made a girl dance with me; on the odd occasions I did dance with a girl, they would say, "Don't touch me, just pretend to be." One time the teacher did make me put my arms round a girl, she made me feel like I was dirt, as soon as the teacher turned away she jumped backwards and literally shuddered and said, "I hate you touching me, you are scruffy." I think that has hurt me more in life than anything else I can think of (apart from a time when I went to Weston-super-Mare and couldn't buy my mom a present). I remember that tune we danced to, even now I can hear it while I am typing up this book – it went, step close, step close, step close, step lar la la… I'm sure you know the rest. I just wanted it to end. I always felt very uncomfortable in that lesson.

All through school I had that treatment off girls, they just did not like sitting by me, they even asked the teacher to move me away from them. When I was in the juniors we were told our class was going to the seaside and we had to save 3d (three pence) a week till we had paid a pound (£1), this took all year. The place we were going to was Weston-super-Mare, but because my mom could not give me 3d every week, it turned out I was the only one not going to the seaside out of my class. A week before they were going I was told to report to the headmaster Mr Taylor; I was worried to death, I was trying to think what I had done wrong. I knocked on his door, I was shaking I can tell you and when he shouted "Come on in" my heart pounded. "Ah, David," he said, "a boy from your class is very poorly and cannot go to Weston next Saturday," (I've tried hard but I can't remember any boy out of my class that didn't go) so his mother told me to give his seat to you and she gave me 2/- (two shillings) for you to spend, so you are going to the seaside with the rest of your class." (I believe now it was Mr Taylor that paid for me to go.) "I have given your teacher the 2/- and she will give it to you on the morning you go on your trip." What kindness those teachers showed and gave to me in the infants and the juniors.

The seniors – that was a whole new ball game, those teachers had a licence to bully children, we thought we were grown-up but we were still children. I can still remember the afternoon we were taken across from the juniors to the seniors to meet the headmaster – as we were going into the seniors after the holidays we were sat in rows in the main hall, on the floor, in walked Mr Bradbury the head of the seniors and for some unknown reason I can see that afternoon like it was yesterday. His first words were, "Good afternoon, boys and girls, you are the big boys and girls of the juniors, after the holidays you will be the little boys and girls of the seniors." That thought sent a shiver down my back, I've no idea why.

Where have the years gone? My mom told me many times enjoy your childhood it's the best years of your life – how right you were, Mother.

BAGS OF RAGS

It's great to be young and to have had the freedom me and Trevor had and the friends I grew up with. Me and Trevor did the most things together. Our other friends got pocket money every week, not much I don't think, me and Trevor didn't at that time.

We had an idea, well it was Trevor's idea really, to go all round our neighbours and ask if they had any old rags. Most people were kind to us, we also asked if they had any woollens they didn't want – talk about cheek, we knew no boundaries, we had no nerves at all, we would do anything to earn money. We were very surprised at the amount we were given because most people in those days wore their clothes till they were threadbare just like we did. After we filled two sacks up and sorted the woollens from the rags we were surprised to find better clothes in there than the ones we were wearing, to be honest we swapped our clothes for ones we had been given as rags. We both now had a new set of clothes and we felt good, even though we never got them washed, well that never bothered me and Trevor – we were used to living in a world of make-do-and-mend.

A boy came up to me one day and took the rise out of me, "That was my jumper, we threw it away because it got a stain under the arm," as he pulled back my coat that had also been someone else's, "see, I told you it was mine, you two are scroungers and scruffy." It was at that moment I realised I wished I was a bully just like he was, me and Trevor were nice gentle boys. I took off that jumper and threw it back in the rag bag, found another jumper in the rag bag and wore that (me and Trevor could have won a fancy dress competition without even getting changed!).

We carried our sacks of rags from Glebe Farm all the way to Cuckoo Bridge Aston to the firm we called Raggy Allans. It took us one and a half hours to walk it; we walked along the 14 bus route through to the Fox and Goose through Washwood Heath then to Aston, the man with the scales would weigh the rags first then the woollens and he would say, "Look, boys, that's what they weigh." I would look but hadn't a clue what I was looking at. "Yes," I would say. He wrote the weight down on a ticket, we then walked past a mountain of rags on either side of us to an office that looked like it belonged in the Dickensian times, a glass window was slid open we handed a faceless person our ticket, out came a hand with our money in it.

We did that walk many times to sell our rags – the ones in the sacks I might add, not the ones we were wearing. We used the money for swimming and bus fares and a cup of Cow & Gate after swimming, we always went Woodcock Street baths. We earned our own money, I think we should feel a little proud of ourselves.

PLAYING GAMES

Games were played every spare minute we children had when we were not running errands, me and my friends played as often as we could, there were six of us and we played every evening in the summer time. I loved the warm summer evenings, the energy we had was endless, we were very fit little fellows, it's only when one gets older you realise just how fit you were, if I had half that energy now I would be happy. These are the games I liked most of all:

Polly on the Mop Stick
Two teams of equal amounts, if there were eight of us we all lined up, we would pick two captains then find an object like a piece of wood or a stone and make one side heads and the other side tails (as none of us had any money, the winning captain would have first pick of the people lined up), we did this for many types of games. To be a mop stick team the leader bends over holding onto the fence with the rest of the team bending forward holding on to the waist of the person in front. The Pollys would run and jump on to the backs of the mop sticks to try and collapse them; the leader of the mop stick had to shout "Polly on the mop stick 1,2,3," and win the game. If the mop stick hadn't collapsed when this was shouted they were the winners and the Pollys had to become the mop sticks. Thinking back now this was a very dangerous game to play.

Kick the Can
This was the same as hide and seek, the only difference was which ever one was on first had to find the ones hiding. We always played this game in the dark. When the person on was looking for the ones hiding, when the ones hiding thought he or she couldn't be seen kicking the can after they had kicked the can they would then run and hide again without being spotted; if the person on saw whoever kicked the can they would shout that person's name and then they would be on if it was correct.

Polly on the Mopstick

This is how we played British Bulldog.

British Bulldog

If any game was dangerous this one was. Again an object would be used for heads and tails to see who would be the Bulldog. Standing on the side of the pavement would be the rest of us, the Bulldog would stand in the middle of the road, the road was laid in concrete, this was in squares so the lines where the concrete finished were the boundaries. Now the Bulldog would shout the name of the person he wished to tackle, and that person had to try to get past the Bulldog and get to the other side of the road, but you weren't allowed to run until the Bulldog shouted "British Bulldog". When the Bulldog tackled you if he got you down on the ground it would be your turn to be the Bulldog. We got a few scratches and bruises trying to get to the other side of the road. One evening a boy named Derek, who never ever played with us asked if he could play; he lived top end of my road, he was very well dressed, "What about your clothes?" I said. "I don't care," he said, "I want to play," "OK you can play," Billy said. Billy was the Bulldog – after two of us had got past Billy, he called out Derek's name, made him wait a while so Derek's adrenalin would be pumping, Billy shouted "British Bulldog," and Derek almost got past him. Billy dived at Derek got his hands round Derek's legs and he went down, hitting his head on the gutter and split his head wide open – the blood flew everywhere and off he ran home. We were told he had sixteen stitches, he never played with us again. Funny to think about it now, we played that game for many a year and scratches was the worst we ever got.

King of The Hill

This was exactly the same as British Bulldog, the only difference was it was played on a hill covered in grass and we could be as rough as we liked on grass.

Hot Rice

Where these names for these games came from I have no idea. We all stood in a ring with clenched fists, using a tennis ball – this was thrown from a clenched fist and caught with a clenched fist. Some people had strong arms and throwing the ball would really hurt. If when thrown to you, you dropped the ball you were on; as soon as the ball was dropped everyone would run. The person that was on had to throw the ball and try to hit the ones running away, if you were hit it was your turn to be on and you had to throw and try to hit someone with the ball, if you sat on a fence or a gate with your feet off the ground the ball could not be thrown at you. We would lie on the floor with our feet in the air and the thrower would stand poised, waiting for your feet to touch the ground; there was a time limit your feet could be off the ground.

Gutter Cricket

With four sticks of wood or lollipop sticks these were placed in the gutter three up right one across the top, same as wickets in cricket. When the ball was thrown if the sticks were knocked down it became the same as hot rice, great fun! It's a shame we had to grow up – ha, ha, my children said I never did.

Famous Stars Initials

This game we played on an old bike – we would ride around in circles, say the first letters of the name of the star to the people standing on the pavement who had to guess the name of the star; whoever guessed the name first got on the bike and rode round in circles, they then had to think of a star's name. The most common ones used were D.D. (Donald Duck, or Diana Dors), M.M. (Mandy Miller or Marilyn Monroe), N.W. (Norman Wisdom), W.H. (Will Hay), O.M.R. (Old Mother Riley). We played for hours, boy we had lots of energy, it's not until you look back over your life you realise just how much.

I Wrote a Letter to My Wife

We all stood round in a circle facing inwards, one person stood outside the circle and ran round the outside saying, "I wrote a letter to my wife and on the way I dropped it," when the words "dropped it" were said, as he or she passed round the outside of the circle, everyone in the circle looked over their shoulder to see if the letter had been dropped behind them; in our case the letter should have been a handkerchief, in our case most times it was a piece of rag, if it had been dropped behind you, you had to pick it up and catch the person that had dropped it before they got back to the space where you had been standing. I loved that game. All the children I grew up with were wonderful. The rhyme we used to say when we were playing this game was:

> I wrote a letter to my wife and on the way I dropped it,
> Somebody must have picked it up and put it in their pocket.
> Thief, thief, drop it, drop it, thief, thief drop it, drop it.

True Dare Kiss or Promise

I liked this game, it was a good laugh. If you said *Kiss*, then you were told who to kiss, if you refused you had to do a forfeit, the person who was on at that time would tell you to do something really daft: like kiss the floor or take your shoes off and run through a puddle, really daft things that gave everyone a good laugh. *Dare* of course meant you were dared to do silly things like diving over a high hedge or surprising one of the girls and telling them you loved them. *True* you were asked something that they knew about you just to see if you would tell the truth, usually they would ask who you were in love with. *Promise* you were told to make a promise, if you didn't keep it they would think of something horrible to do to you, like get you in trouble with your mom or a neighbour, we really did have some great times playing this game. Oh to be young again.

Football

When we were playing football one day outside Johnny's house I kicked the ball and it came off the side of my foot and smashed a window in Johnny's house. I had to pay 6d (sixpence every week) till I paid for it and ran errands to save the money up. I was very careful after that.

Playing my favourite game – Football

THINK OF A NUMBER BELOW TEN (DON'T TELL ME WHAT IT IS)

DOUBLE IT, ADD FOUR, HALVE IT, TAKE AWAY THE FIRST NUMBER YOU THOUGHT OF, YOU ARE LEFT WITH NUMBER 2

Do you remember this puzzle? Everyone did these types of puzzles.

DID YOU?

ONE IN THE EYE

One very cold winter's day me and my friends were playing in the horse road, the snow had started to melt but was still sort of frozen – when rolled in the hands it was snow mixed with ice, water would be running through the fingers when rolled as a snow ball. We all agreed we wouldn't throw this mixture of snow and ice at each other, only at cans or objects that we stood up in the hedge.

I had been sliding down the hill, and after an hour my feet were soaking wet; pumps that were worn out with almost no sole on them is not the best footwear in the middle of winter. Billy, a friend of mine, decided to start throwing those ice and snowballs at us, "Come on, Billy," we all shouted, "we've agreed we wouldn't throw the ice it's dangerous." He was laughing, "Come on, you girls, I thought you were tough boys." "Now look, Billy," I was saying, and as I turned round an ice ball hit me in both eyes. The pain was unbearable, I thought I had lost my sight, all my mates shouted, "Billy you idiot, you've blinded Dave."

Billy was really frightened. I was without my eyesight for about nine days – doctors, hospital – all because Billy couldn't resist throwing snowballs. I was off school for two weeks, and when I returned to school I was taken to the headmaster's office, well frog-marched would be the right way to describe it. I was poked and pushed and called a liar, nothing I said would be believed. "You think I'm stupid don't you, snowballs in your eyes, you were playing truant weren't you?" said the headmaster. "No, Sir," I answered. "Don't you no Sir me, my lad," the head went on. It really upset me, I never did have days off school for no reason, I had really suffered with my eyes. That's one of the reasons I hated going to school, I always did go, I wouldn't have but my mother made me.

MINE OR YOUR MOM'S

It's hard to imagine that these days that a family of six, (four children, two adults) could be living in a house with no food in the house anywhere not even a crust of bread to eat or any coal or wood to burn to heat the house. That's how we lived for many a year. There were times of course when we would seem to have enough to eat but not often enough, I don't think.

In the 1950s almost everyone got paid on a Friday, but Trevor's dad Fred got paid on a Thursday – he worked in the wholesale fruit market in the centre of Birmingham. Well, my mom used to make me look out of the living room window to tell her when Fred was coming down the road. "He's coming, Mom," I would shout. "Give him five minutes to get into the house then go and ask him if he will lend me 2/6d (that's half a crown)." He always lent my mom money on a Thursday, and after I took the money back to my mom she would send me up the road to the shops for a loaf, potatoes and sometimes Spam from Braggs the cake shop (some of my relatives worked for Mr Bragg himself during the war, one of them being my Auntie Maggie, being so short of sugar she helped herself and took sugar home in her handbag. Mr Bragg went to my granddad's and asked him to have a word with his daughter – Granddad was none too pleased as he was unaware of what had been going on. My Auntie Maggie was killed during a bombing raid. I would like to have known my Auntie Maggie. All this information was passed on to me by my eldest brother. The family lived at number 20 or 30 Ashe Road, Saltley). The money borrowed off Fred, I did this week after week (poor man), it went to 5/- (five shillings), then finally it went to 10/- (ten shillings). My mom always made me ask for the money.

It wasn't always doom and gloom, sometimes life seemed wonderful. I think maybe the winters were the hardest times, coal had to be bought, extra gas used and we seemed to eat more in the winter. One Thursday I went to borrow 10/- for my mom and

Trevor's dad said, "I'm not sure who owns this 10/- me or your mother," but as a true friend he never said no. I never knew why Trevor's poverty was as bad as mine because his dad worked very hard, up at four every morning to the market. Maybe his pay was poor. My mom always paid him back his 10/- Friday evenings without fail. My dad got paid on a Friday so some Fridays I was told to go and meet Dad outside his works at 1.00 p.m. dinner time – he would come out and give me a 10/- note and 2d for my bus fare back home and he moaned every time, his cus words were "Gad blimey". When I got home my mom would send me to the shops up the road to buy some food items, I was fit in those days I can tell you.

THURSDAY PICTURES

Trevor's mom and my mom went to the pictures most Thursday evenings, the cinema was called the Atlas. It was the only couple of hours our moms had on their own – their bit of quality time without kids around them. One Thursday afternoon I had a bright idea – I will scrub the kitchen floor, (they were red quarry tiles) when she sees what I have done she will be delighted and take me to the pictures with her. So I got scrubbing with a big green bar of fairy soap and a worn-out scrubbing brush. I filled a bucket half full of water and threw the water on to the floor, flooding the kitchen. After I had scrubbed half the floor, right, I thought now I will tell Mom what I am doing and pictures here I come. I went round the house shouting, "Mom, Mom." My sister said, "Mom's gone to the pictures with Trevor's mom." What a shock that was, I was horrified – she had slipped out of the front door and never closed it so I wouldn't know she had gone. I left the kitchen floor swimming in water and ran over the road to see Trevor.

"Trev, Trev," I shouted, "they've gone to the pictures without us knowing, let's run down Audley Road – we might get there before they do." We ran non stop till we reached the picture house and watched two buses go by. "We've missed them, Trev," I said, "that kitchen floor – my sister will go mad at me." She was hopping mad, she had to mop all that water up I had left. I never made that mistake again, I left scrubbing floors to my mom. Mom used to scrub that floor on her hands and knees, then put newspaper down, we had to jump from one page to another, we dare not step on the floor. This paper was left down until the floor was dry and by this time the paper was all dirty and ripped with us kids running in with our dirty pumps on. If she had enough pennies in the gas metre she would light the oven to dry the floor quicker but that didn't happen too often, as she said with 3d (three pence) she could feed her children so the floor could dry on its own.

COACH TRIP

Trevor came to me one day with what I thought was a brilliant idea. He had seen an advert in our local post office, Bowens a coach company were doing coach trips to a place called Leamington – this town had the whole place lit up, on the advert it said Leamington lights. “Shall we go there, Dave?” Trevor said. “Where is it, Trev?” I asked. “I don’t know, Dave, it sounds good though doesn’t it.” “Yeah,” I replied, so off to Bowens to see how much it cost – 3/6 for children I think it was (three shillings and six pence). “Right, Trev, we will have to run lots of errands to get the 7/- (seven shillings) we need.” “And we will need some spending money, Dave, we had better start right away,” said Trevor. “Yeah OK, Trev,” I replied.

We worked really hard; we went back to knocking on doors for old rags and pop bottles, we fetched coal for our moms and neighbours, quarter hundred weight at a time, we never charged our moms, we made two shillings 2/- fetching coal. We got up early to fit in all the errands we had agreed to do the day before, and we worked hard for two weeks but we did it. We only had a 1/- (one shilling) to spend plus our 3d (three pence) bus fare back home.

The coach company wasn’t far from our houses so we walked there, it only took twenty minutes to walk, that way we saved 3d bus fare. As we walked into the office a very pretty young lady greeted us, I was staring at her she was so pretty, suddenly Trevor gave me a nudge and said, “She’s talking to you.” “Sorry, lady,” I said, “but you are the prettiest lady I have ever seen.” With a big smile she thanked me, “Now, boys, can I help you?” “Can we book two seats please to see the lights, at um… where is it, Trev?” “I can’t remember, Dave.” “It must be Leamington lights you mean, boys.” We both said, “Yeah that’s it, lady.”

We got the coach at 7.00 p.m., I remember that but where it picked us up from for the life of me I can’t remember, neither can

Trevor. You know not once did anyone ask "where are your parents?" or "who are you with?" I have a good memory but those lights are not very clear in my mind, I do remember looking for a fish and chip shop, after what seemed a long time we found one, after all that walking we were hungry and thirsty. It was a warmish night I remember, good job because our pumps had holes in the bottom. Our socks we could not pull up because they were tucked under our feet to keep our feet from getting sore from the pavement. Both me and Trevor only had jumpers on as at that time we did not possess coats. My mom bought all my clothes from the jumble sales and so did Trevor's mom. We weren't the cleanest two little boys in the city but no one passed any comments. The chips we bought were 4d (four pence) a packet. I was very surprised to see the chips as they were crinkle chips, I had never seen crinkled chips before. We had bought a bottle of pop and shared it. The chips seemed to be hollow inside, I did not like them at all but I ate them because by this time we were both starving.

So back on the coach and to our surprise we were dropped off in the middle of Birmingham city centre. We had saved 3d for our bus fare home. Town was absolutely deserted, I had never seen it like it, it was like a ghost town. We had no idea it would be so late, we weren't told and as young boys the time never entered our heads, we were just excited to be on our first coach trip. The one thing we had never thought about because we didn't know we were going to be dropped off in the middle of town, is that after midnight the bus fares doubled. We tried to tell the bus conductor a sad story but he would not have any of it. He told us to clear off. "Please, Mister," I said, "it's a long way home and I only have 3d." He replied, "I told you NO, clear off." He rang the bell and off the bus went and we were left there standing. I hope his son gets better treatment from people than he gave to us.

So we had about an eight or nine mile walk. It was creepy, not a soul to be seen anywhere. We got to the fire station in Gosta Green. It was getting quite chilly at this time as we were still in short trousers and no coats. As we passed the gun shop called Webley and Scott there were two police officers in the doorway – boy did they have a shock, because we were wearing pumps they didn't hear us coming. A policeman and a police woman, such a scuffle, the lady police officer was attempting to pull down her skirt and the male officer adjusting his dress. He came from the doorway sounding very cross then he said, "What on earth are you young boys doing out at this time of night?" We explained we had not got enough bus fare to get home and that the conductor would not let us on the bus and we were walking back home. "Does your mom know that you are out at this time of night?" "Yes," I replied. I really thought I was going to get a ride in a police car and be taken home (well I was hoping). With a wave of his hand he said, "Hurry up and get home, it's getting late." After saying that he went straight back into the doorway, I had not got a clue what they were doing.

My mom had no idea what time I got in, she knew where I had been. She was never worried about me at all as she knew I could be trusted. She did ask if we enjoyed ourselves. I said, "Yes," but didn't tell her we had walked home from town at midnight. I asked Trevor if his mom knew what time he got in. He said she never missed him

I wonder would you let your children do all the things we did?

HELPING BROTHER

My eldest brother was in the R.E.M.E. as a regular soldier with only six months to demob from the army. He was sent to Korea to fight; he was there eighteen months, and when he returned he was very ill suffering with T.B. and Pleurisy. After coming out of hospital he had to find ways of making extra money so he started looking for scrap metal, in those days people used to dump their old cars on any piece of waste ground. Donald used to take the radiators off these old cars because they were made of copper and brass – after fighting for his country that's what he had to do to pay his rent.

At that time the National Assistant Board visited Donald, looked round his house – all he and his wife possessed was a bed, a table and two chairs. The visitor told him he was comfortable and he was offered 1/- (one shilling) a week which, added to his sick pay, was not even enough to pay his rent. Donald told him what to do with his shilling and ordered him out of his house as he was too ill to throw him out physically. Thank you, England, that's where I come in.

Back to the tip looking for metal, I did well out of that tip, Donald gave me a magnet and said any metal that doesn't stick to it put in the sack, bring the sack to me and I will give you half a crown (2/6d). So I called for Trevor, told him, and he couldn't wait to get started. The tip was the same tip we always went to at the back of the Atlas Cinema; we spent some hours on that tip, talk about Mud Larks, we were the Tip Rats. After taking the filled sack to Donald, "I will weigh it in tomorrow if I feel a little better, so I will pay you then the next day," he said.

Each day we went to the tip, there was new rubbish arriving all the time, one day was very good, we filled our sack quite quick so off to brother's with the bag of tat. "Here you are, lads, three shillings for that bag of tat yesterday and half a crown for this sack today. Get me another sack full like this one you brought today and I will give you two shillings and sixpence for the next bag."

Trevor and me went swimming the next day, the money was burning a hole in our pockets, we only earned money so we could go swimming and to the pictures (cinema). The baths was in Woodcock Street near Birmingham city centre. Very next day we were back on the tip, we had filled one and a half sacks with tat when a very rough looking man came over to us and shouted at us and swore, he took our sacks and said, "These are mine now, now clear off this is my patch." We had never seen him before, he was rough and he terrified us both. "Trev, I'm not letting him steal our tat, I'm going to get it back when he goes down the side of the tip. I'm going to run over there and get our sacks back." As I was stronger than Trevor, I said, "I will grab our two sacks, you grab his sack." When the man went down the side of the tip, we ran over grabbed our sacks and he heard us and tried to get back up quickly but he kept sliding down. We were running as fast as we could, he was shouting after us, language I had never heard before. Needless to say we never went back to that tip, for a couple of weeks anyway; doesn't mean we stopped earning money, no way, we came up with all sorts of ideas. We got five shillings for those three bags of tat off my brother.

Donald changed his tactics from tatting to selling door-to-door; he decided to go to a warehouse and buy various items that he thought would sell. Things like American comics, toys, combs, little boy dolls about two inches tall with a rubber dunce's hat on which when filled with water you squeezed the hat the doll weed. Donald asked me and Trevor if we would go door-to-door to sell these items for him, and we were excited at the thought of earning extra money. It was three comics for a shilling, I remember one of the comics was called *Little Sheriff*; three combs for a shilling – pink green and blue, I sold dozens of these. I was becoming a proper little salesman. When I was asked where did you get those from I said the same thing every time, "I'm selling them for my brother he's just come back from Korea, he's been fighting in the army and he is very ill with T.B. and PLEURISY." This was the truth, he was very sick for a very long time and I liked helping him and every shilling I made he gave me 2d (two pence) for helping him, people were very kind. When he got fed up selling these items from the warehouse he started to buy old cars to cut up and tat in.

I must say that selling door-to-door taught me how to deal with the public. I became a salesman not long after I left school.

THE BOYS' BRIGADE

Joining the Boys' Brigade was an organisation I loved being part of. We always met up one evening a week; they had a football team, and at that time in my life all I lived for was football so I joined their team. I was asked what position I played, when I said in goal they were overjoyed. When I played in our first game I realised why they were happy to have someone who had a little football skill. They were absolutely useless, we lost every match we played. I saved dozens of what would have seemed cert goals but we always lost, never less than (if my memory serves me right) sixteen nil, normally it was twenty or more. As they thought I was good they made me captain. I'm sure if there was a cup for the worst team in England's history we would have been famous, well we were in the papers as the team that likes losing twenty nil on a regular basis.

I remember one game very well, we were twenty-two to nil down, I got so fed up I came out of my goal, dribbled the ball, got past them all, I got to the goalie, he hadn't touched the ball all through the match, he must have been stiff from having nothing to do. I scored so we lost twenty-two to one. I bet that goalie hated me, the only time he had to make a save he missed, saving only by an inch but he missed, it was more luck than skill on my part. All part of growing up. I really enjoyed being part of the team even though we lost every game.

This Boys' Brigade met in the Lea Village area of Birmingham in a school known as Ridpool Road School. We had to march to church on the last Sunday of the month. I only had part of the uniform, I was the only one that wore pumps as I didn't have any shoes and that was accepted, no one ever said anything I'm glad to say; I would have loved to have worn the same as everyone else but that wasn't to be. However, I was very happy there. Happy times.

SCOUTS

The Scouts was also happy times for me. At the top of my road, across the main road this was Audley Road, to the right was St. Andrews Church – it was in this church where the Boy Scouts held their meetings once a week. I tried to join several times but was always told there was a waiting list of two years.

One evening as I was passing the church I noticed the Scouts were outside recognising different birds and naming them, well I thought I would try my luck, so I went up to the leader and asked him if I could join. "You've tried before haven't you?" he said. "Many times," I replied. "OK," he said to my delight, "fill in this form and I will enrol you. Would you like to stay and join in the activities this evening?" I was asked. "Yes please," I replied. "Right, sit in with that group sitting on the floor, they are being taught how to tie knots," I was told by the Scout leader. I was over the moon with excitement, "Thank you very much," I replied, I was so happy. He shook my hand and said, "Welcome to the Scout movement."

I told Trevor but he didn't want to join so I tried very hard to get some money together. I ran errands with Trevor, and when I had earned three shillings I went to the Scouts shop in Birmingham city centre; I bought a woggle, the next week I bought the neckerchief, I never did get any other parts of the uniform, a cap or jumper, and at that time I was the only one that hadn't got a full uniform. I was asked by one of the boys a few times, "How did you get to join, my friend has been waiting nearly two years to get in to our group?" In the end I told him a little white lie, I said, "I had been waiting over two years to join."

I really loved being part of that group. We sometimes went to some woods called Yorkswood, sadly it is now a housing estate. We used to have paper chases, wild animal recognition and tree recognition, these woods were on the border of Shard End area. I loved all that, I was useless at it but I enjoyed it. We marched to church the last Sunday in the month as did all those kinds of groups did in those days. We were expected to visit church every Sunday and were asked why not if we didn't attend. I loved to march with the band playing, I felt proud to be part of it all, to see the Sea Cadets, the Girl Guides, the Brownies, the Cubs and the Scouts all marching together was for me a wonderful sight.

I was part of that Scout movement for fifteen months or so. It would be nice to see the children marching these days and belonging to a group of one sort or another, of course in those days most of us didn't have a TV and computers were non existent. After I left the Scout movement I joined the Sea Cadets. Trevor never did join any of these groups with me.

THE SEA CADETS

In the same year I left the Scouts I joined the Sea Cadets. There on the parade ground, all in groups of about thirty, there must have been about one hundred and fifty Cadets, I only stuck it for four weeks, they didn't seem to do much. I never got any part of the uniform plus it just didn't appeal to me. I thought we would be sailing on the reservoir, that seemed rare, so I packed up that group.

I joined the Baptist Church confessed all my sins and became a Born Again Christian. I loved all the people that were part of the Baptist movement, even the girls talked to me – that was a shock, girls normally looked down their noses at me but not those girls they were wonderful. That's the only time in my life that girls treated me nice, mind you it never stopped me hating girls.

I must add when confessing my sins the Preacher was surprised I hadn't sinned at all apart from scrumping apples. Still believing in Our Lord, but do not attend church anymore.

TWO BLACK POODLES

While sitting on my front garden wall one fine sunny morning, wondering what I should do that day to earn some money so I could go swimming, while I was deep in thought, thinking I ran errands yesterday for Mrs R, so she won't want any, when I suddenly nearly left my skin. Trevor had crept round the back of me and shouted down my ear – boy that broke my train of thought. He said, "Come on, Dave, let's go to town." "I've no money, Trevor," I replied. "It's OK, I will pay your fare, my dad just gave me some money," answered Trevor.

So on the bus we go through Stechford, then the Pelham, Alum Rock, Saltley, Nechells, Gosta Green, then town, Birmingham – it was about thirty-five minutes – the terminus was called the Old Square. Trevor's dad worked in the fruit market, he worked there from a boy; we walked to St. Martins church, where there was a barrow boy, we bought some damsons off him 3d (three pence) a bag but when we opened the bag to eat the damsons they were all rotten. We went back and complained – all the words he used I can't print! They went straight into the bin – 3d to us was an hour or more running errands, I could never treat children the way me and Trevor were treated.

We went to the rag market, it was packed; as we were walking round we passed a stall were they sold crockery called Lees where I spotted in a box two black Poodles, in the begging position with glass eyes, they looked beautiful, they were made of chalk they were 1/11d (one and eleven pence) for the two. I asked the man if he would save them for me till next week, he said, "Yes," but I didn't think he would for one minute. "Can you make them any cheaper?" I asked him, I will leave his reply to your imagination. Trevor asked, "What do you want them for, Dave?" I answered him with, "Well, Trev, we were selling all those things for my brother if you remember I thought we could go all round the houses and raffle them." Trevor's reply was, "Cor, Dave, what a brilliant idea."

So all the next week we ran errands and saved all the money we had earned, we didn't even go swimming. Come Saturday morning we went early to town we thought the poodles were so good someone might buy them (well we were only children). Trevor said, "Don't ask him for them cheaper, Dave, he might not sell them to us." "Trev, after what he said to me last Saturday I don't think I will." I bought the dogs, "Right, Trev, we need a raffle book now," I said. We found one on a stall for 3d (three pence), and when we got back home (about one o'clock) we started in Trevor's road went down one side back up the other selling the tickets for 6d (sixpence) each. Trevor was holding the poodles up so they could see them.

We were known to most people because we had sold them comics, dolls, combs, toys. I did all the talking, and when I was asked who gave you permission to sell door-to-door I told a little white lie – I said they were being raffled for my brother who was very ill because he had been fighting in the army in Korea and now was in hospital. That was the truth about my brother, but the raffle that was for me and Trevor. They were happy to buy tickets because they thought they were helping an injured soldier who had been fighting for his country. Well, we were threatened with the police, told to bugger off, called scruffy little urchins, and one or two things I can't repeat. The one that stayed in my mind, a woman threw her arms in the air, went hysterical and shouted, "Get away, get away those are made of chalk, it's unlucky, get away from my house," and slammed the door in our faces. We sold two pounds five shillings' worth of tickets then stopped selling. People did ask how would they know who had won, I told them we would go round and tell everyone. They all put their name and addresses on the stub of the tickets; we did intend to go round but never did.

We sat in my mom's kitchen and I said, "Who shall we give them to, Trev, shall we give them to Mrs G – she is as poor as we are?" Trevor answered, "Yeah, Dave," so off we went. She only lived at the top of my road, we knocked on the door, her son opened the door and in a very stern voice he said, "Yes?" I told him, "You have won the raffle." His face lit up, "Mother, Mother," he shouted, "We've won the raffle, thanks boys." As I walked away I felt good inside, we had made someone happy. People were stopping us for a week afterwards asking who had won and why did you not come and tell us – we did but no one was in, that's what we told them all who asked us. We could have kept those dogs and no one would have known, well *we* would have done. We were very honest young boys keeping them never entered our head.

Earning our pocket money.
“Buy a raffle ticket, Lady?”

LEAGUE CHAMPIONS

In the juniors school I played football, and at that time it was my life I played centre forward. 1955 was a magic year for me when we won the League Championship. I was coached by my teacher Mr Lycehart, I liked this teacher, he was very good to me. I enjoyed my time in the juniors and I was sorry to leave and go into the seniors.

While in the juniors I also used to do high jumping, I was high jump champion all through my school days, juniors and seniors, because I had a good spring in my legs. The teacher, Mr Green, who was my teacher in the seniors, I didn't like him very much, he was my sports teacher and when I was doing my school work he used to hit me across the back of the head, pick me up out of my chair by my hair and sometimes by my ear, that was the worst, by my ear. I was hopeless at my school work and I was punished for it. I left school not being able to spell or read very well, but in sports I was OK, I could hold my own.

Mr Green thought he would try me in goal, I soon found out that was the position for me, I loved playing in goal. Our team in the seniors at Audley Road School, we never won a trophy but it was great to play football. Mr Green praised my sporting abilities but slapped me about when it came to my school work. To be stood up in the school hall when in assembly and praised by the Headmaster for my achievements in sport for the school, if I'm honest it gave me a big head at times. Well, to be told how useless you are nearly every day – it makes you feel good when told you are the best the school has when it comes to sport. When told things like this at times it can give a child a big head.

Author back row, second in from the right.
1955 was a special year for me
Mr Lyceheart, the teacher

The one thing I was good at was high jumping.
I was school champion all through my school days.

Author is second from right in back row, wearing my football shirt, having had my photo taken five minutes before with the football team and told to leave the shirt on for this photo.

BULLYING

I was born with a perforated ear drum, I suffered with itching ears all the time. I had to attend the school clinic once a week and I was accused by the Headmaster of crying wolf. I was a small boy needing treatment and refused because grown-ups know best – not this time. When my ear started running I was taken to the Headmaster's office to show him. "Please, Sir, may I go to the clinic for treatment." I was waiting for a slap across the head or the cane and to my surprise he looked and said. "So you weren't crying wolf after all? OK, you can go, here is a note for the clinic."

So off I went, feeling very good because I was getting off school. As I walked into the clinic, brother those nurses were rougher than the teachers. I was ordered about just as though I had been naughty. I never was – as a child I was always afraid of being punished, well I was punished by my teachers all the time because I was stupid (as I was always being told). I just couldn't remember anything I was taught the day before so I was pushed, poked, shook and slapped daily. The nurses had taken lessons from the teachers I reckon. Before I went in to see the doctor they shouted to me to sit in the chair; not knowing which chair, I was frog-marched and pushed (well, thrown) into the chair. When the nurse started poking my ear, rough – she couldn't have been any rougher if she had used a shovel. The pain was making me cry. "Shut up, you baby." When it felt like she had cut my ear off, the blood ran down my face. She thrust a tissue into my hand, "Here hold that to your ear, now go and see the doctor," she growled.

As I walked in a very surprised look came over the doctor's face. "And what have you been up to, young man?" "That nurse did it," I said. "Oh," that's all he said. After he stopped the bleeding, drops were put in my ear and a wad of cotton wool pushed hard into my ear, even that was giving me pain. Nothing else was ever done, it was for me to suffer, children just did not count in those days. It was at that clinic that I found I had been born with a perforated ear drum, and to this day still it troubles me. As I walked out of the doctor's room I passed a nurse ordering some other poor boy about. I never did get a sorry or an apology, nothing, just a "Go on hurry back to school."

Back in school I went straight to my classroom and was greeted with, "Where have you been?" with a slap on the back of my head and ordered to sit down. With my ear giving me pain, now the back of my head had pain, and with cotton wool in my hearing was only functioning at about 40%. Trying to do my writing I didn't hear the teacher shouting at me to pay attention, next thing was the blackboard rubber came flying across the classroom. Just at that moment I looked up, because by this time the teacher was screaming at me, I looked up just to see what all the noise was about, the blackboard rubber glanced just off my right eyebrow, right next to my eye – a quarter of an inch nearer it would have damaged my eye. So now I had a bad ear, a headache, and a lump on my right eyebrow. I was ordered to pay attention and to bring back the blackboard rubber to the teacher. On doing this I was slapped again on the back of my head, ordered to go and sit down and pay attention in the future. I wonder if I met that teacher now I'm 65 (at the time of writing) slapped him on the back of his head, grabbed him by his lapels and shook him violently – there wouldn't be any difference would there? He slapped me about when I was defenceless, at his age now I would get locked up, which he should have been for knocking me about. A defenceless child. I really would like to meet him to tell him what a rotten teacher he was. I was so afraid of him, I just couldn't concentrate on my school work which meant I learnt nothing; in turn this led to being slapped across the back of my head for not knowing how to do any lessons. I left school not knowing the difference between signature and initials.

DOWN AND OUT

It was one Saturday morning I saw my mate John walking down the path to my house, I was coming back from the shops having done some shopping for my mom. With a very loud voice I shouted to him, "I've been looking for you." He said, "Guess what – na, don't think I should tell you." "Go on, go on, John, what is it?" I said. "I have joined the Morris Commercial boxing club," he replied. "Yo ain't?" I questioned. "I have – honest," he replied, "I went with a boy from my school who was already a member of the boxing club." John is a Catholic, I'm Church of England so we both attended different schools. I hadn't seen John the evening before that's why I disbelieved him, he always told me everything he did so I was very surprised when he told me, "Honest, Dave, I asked the trainer if he would let you join," said John. "Bet he said no," I replied. "Well," said John, with a sad looking face and looking down at the floor, in a soft voice he said, "I was told to bring you along Tuesday evening."

Well I was so excited I jumped up and down and shouted, "Yeah, yeah!" John said, "I thought you would be pleased." "Oh thanks, John, for asking for me, I'll start training right away," I answered with great excitement, so we started to run what we called round the square, that was up my road, along Audley Road, past the row of ten shops then down Swancote Road till we reached my road and repeated it many times over. We were shadow boxing all the time we were running – boy did I have some grand ideas! About the third time around I was going to be world champion; I'm fit and strong, I was telling myself.

After we had stopped running I was by my garden gate, still shadow boxing, I must have looked a right idiot, Trevor came over to me, "What are you doing?" he asked. "I'm training, Trev," I answered. "What for, Dave?" questioned Trevor. "I'm going to be a boxer," the whole time I was talking to him I was shadow boxing, "John has joined the boxing club down Alum Rock and he has got me in, I will ask for you Trev," I told him. "Na, I don't want to box, our Tony went there some time ago," Trevor said. So I went with Trevor to talk with his brother Tony, he said he liked it but just stopped going, "Try it, Dave, you will like it," he said.

So come Tuesday evening, I think that was the night, might have been Thursday evening – any road up, I started at the boxing club. I was training with a medicine ball, after that we all did road work, that's running round the streets. I felt good, my ideas of becoming a champion grew even stronger. I did all this for a few weeks even did some sparing in the ring with older boys. I held my own, mind you they weren't hitting to hurt, only getting me used to the feel of the ring. After a few months I had my first bout; a visiting team came, it was only a friendly so we could gain more experience – my turn came, three rounds, three minutes each round, out I came for the first round I was quicker than my opponent, I jabbed with my left, I only threw my right once, I remember he never laid a glove on me. Yeah, I thought, this is easy, I am going to win this fight, end of round one. The trainer was well pleased with me, he said, "Just keep doing what you are doing, it's in the bag." Round two, out I went really cocky if I'm honest, my opponent came out, hit me with a left hook and knocked me out with one punch, I'm ashamed to say. I was out for nearly three hours, not knocked out completely but not able to stand on my own two feet, that day was the end of my boxing career. Some champion eh?

101… 102… 103… I don't think he wants to play any more.

OUR PARK

Glebe Farm park is in Birmingham, I spent many hours in that park. The River Cole runs through that park, and on the edge of the park there is an alleyway that runs the whole of the length of it; at one end of the alleyway there is a road called Colehall Lane, at the other end is Bushberry Road, half way up the alleyway is a very big tree. I have no idea what type of tree it is, we used to have rope tied to that tree and swing across the river, most of the boys that lived around Glebe Farm and Shard End used to play by the river.

One dry day we were playing on the swing, my friend Trevor and me, when a bully boy came up to us and told us to get of the swing as he was now going to use it. Me and Trevor weren't bullies at our young age, I suppose you could call us cowards, well to be very honest at that time in our lives we were cowards, yes for sure we were. The bully got hold of the rope, ran in a circle went sailing through the air shouting, "Yeah, yeah, this is great I haven't done this in a long time." He was very well dressed, well in those days everyone seemed well dressed to me and Trevor. He went across the river two times, on the third time as he was coming back across the river the rope snapped; the river was quite deep at that time, and he disappeared under the water which looked very dirty. We stood on the bank laughing and shouting abuse at him, only because we felt safe where we were and knew he wouldn't be in the mood to chase us, well I did say we were cowards. We shouted as we were running away, "We are glad you went into the water," Trevor said, "Ay, Dave, I hope we don't bump into him again." "Cor and I do, Trev, I'm staying away for a while, Trev," I said. "Yeah me too, Dave," Trevor agreed.

We never did see him again, that bully boy. A long time after that we did go to that tree where we all played swinging across the river, this time we were with our other friends Billy, Johnny,

Eddy, but Dougie wasn't with us that day. As we approached the big tree with the swing, there were lots of lads from our school playing on it, and just as one boy went to swing across the river the rope snapped. Fortunately he didn't go into the river; as he clung to the side of the river bank to save himself from falling in he shouted, "Has anybody got a decent rope?" Billy suddenly shouted, "Yes I've got a rope, it's a great big thick one, it's that thick it will carry ten men but I want it back when you've finished with it." They all shouted, "Go on, Bill, get it now."

Billy asked me if I'd go home with him to get the rope, he needed help to carry it; he told me it was his dad's rope. It was a black tar rope and very thick. "Wow!" all the boys gasped when they saw the rope that would hold ten men. Up the tree Billy went, it took a while before he caught the rope, so already by this time there were about sixteen lads, all wanting to be first. Alan Blackwell's brother (whose name I can't recall) won first go by picking the shortest straw. He took a good run and swung across the river, when the rope snapped and into the river he fell, he scrambled out dripping wet. All he said as he walked off home was, "Ten men," and he disappeared across the park. He didn't have very far to walk as his house backed onto the park.

I was pushed into the river at that same spot many times – we never learn, well I didn't that's for sure. I went to that same spot to collect grass with a boy named Reg. I never ever played with him and was surprised one day when he asked me to help him pick grass for his rabbits. Near the river where the swing used to be were spiked railings, inside there was long lush green grass – we climbed over the railings, we then picked quite a big bagful. Reg suddenly threw the bag over the fence and shouted, "Dave, come on quick, get over the railings." I became very frightened seeing the look on his face, and his hurried actions. I got over those railings much quicker than when I went in I can tell you. Reg ran much faster than me, he was about three years older; when we reached the road puffing, panting and our lungs screaming for air I finally got my words out and asked him what the matter was. What he told me worried me for a long time afterwards, he said there was a man creeping up on us on his belly. It took me a long time to go back to that place again.

When we played on those rope swings they of course got worn out very quickly and eventually would break. We never knew where all those ropes came from but I will for sure remember that thick black tar rope of Billy's the most. To this day it brings a smile to my face whenever I think about it.

CYCLING

Going to Kenilworth Castle on our bikes, we did this many times, one occasion stands out in my mind far more than any other. Once again it was a warm sunny morning, I'm sitting on my front garden gate when Johnny came down the road from the shops, he had run an errand for someone. He shouted very loudly, "Hi Pross," he was always very loud, one of those boys you could hear and pick out in a crowd and know exactly where he was. He asked, "What you doing today?" "Nunk," I answered.

I always used that common word "nunk", meaning of course "nothing". Thinking about it, all or nearly all my speech was in common Brummie slang, I had quite forgotten about it. Words such as nunk, nowt spondulucks, akers, 2/6 two and a kick, 5/- a dollar, 10/- half a bar, 10/- half a sheet, a sheet £1 a wonna, 6d tanner, ain't, wunt, gob bin yow sharnt – gosh so many of us boys had our own language and many more slang words like bin means going a dolla 5/-. I think I would need another lifetime to write them all down.

"I thought we could go to Kenilworth Castle," Johnny said. "I'm game," so off we went to call on our other mates Trevor, Billy and Eddie; all agreed, we set off half an hour later. None of us had any money or food or water to take with us – we never did, we lived like this all the time. Looked after each other, did whatever we could to survive. From Glebe Farm, Stechford, Birmingham 33 to Kenilworth Castle seemed a very long way, I drive it now in the car and I always say the same thing – how on earth as young lads on bikes with no food or water did we do a long run like this and we did it many times.

I remember going across Stonebridge, on the way to Kenilworth, it was just a country lane then, now a major road. All riding together, if we saw blackberries we would pick some, damsons, apples, swedes, carrots from the farmer's field, we only took what we could eat, no more, never destroyed anything and of course it depended on the time of year what we ate. It usually took us about an hour and a half to two hours to reach the Castle depending on how many stops we made.

The Castle was wrapped up in scaffolding. We walked with our bikes round the outside of the Castle and always picked a spot where we could climb over the wall – we did this every time, well we couldn't pay to go in as none of us had a penny to our name. First place we headed for was the water tap, thinking back now I can't remember where it was situated, what I do remember was whoever was drinking the ones waiting for a drink would be saying, "Come on, hurry up we all want a drink." When we were all watered (I would like to say and fed but alas water was all we had), we would climb and investigate the ruins. Billy who was very daring very skinny and wiry decided to climb to the top of the scaffolding, he got right to the top and started jumping and screaming, "I'm the king of the Castle," at that he jumped to a scaffold bar but couldn't hold on.

He fell and hit every bar on the way down, those bars being rough were like rubbing sandpaper on one's skin, every bar he hit took skin off some part of his body. He hit the ground with a thud. It took five minutes for him to come round, and when he did all we could hear was moans and groans, he was in a state. Fortunately he hadn't any broken bones, so we all climbed back over the wall where we had left our bikes and walked back to the road. By now Billy had recovered but was badly bruised, battered, skinless and very sore. He was just about to get on his bike when two cyclists stopped, the lady asked, "What happened to you?" We all told her, she was very sympathetic took out her first aid kit and cleaned him up, she was very thoughtful, what kindness she showed.

We returned to Kenilworth Castle a few times after that, but none of us ever climbed on the scaffolding especially not Billy.

My friends and I at Kenilworth Castle

PAPER BOY

When I was 13 years old I got a paper round, 13/- (thirteen) shillings a week. I went to Hunts Radio Shop where they also sold bikes and bought a bike on H.P. (hire purchase) and paid for it out of my paper round money. My mom had to sign for it of course as I was too young to take out hire purchase agreements. It was a Raleigh.

I adored a girl named Carol, I suppose it was puppy love at the age of 14 years old, this girl lived in the road opposite the paper shop who I delivered papers for. On the way home from school we took a short cut through an alleyway, this alleyway ran through a field known as the home guard field. It was in this field I had my first kiss and cuddle, it was very passionate or so it seemed at that time.

The next day at school I plucked up the courage to ask her to be my girl and go out with me, she smiled and said, "Yes." Every day I walked her to her road, but she was adopted and her adopted father forbade her to have anything to do with lads.

After walking her to her road one day as I was on my way to the paper shop, I stood talking to Carol at the top of her road, when a gaze of total fear came into her eyes, "It's my dad," she said trembling. He was a little white-haired man, slightly bent forward in a raging temper. I was slightly nervous, I just waited there to say hello to him, just to prove to him everything was OK because I knew how over-protective he was as Carol had previously told me. Just as I was about to say hello, without a word his right hand came round and gave me one almighty slap around the face which hurt my ear. Instinctively I swung my right fist at him, fortunately I missed, but as he walked away slapping Carol round the head, in a hurt rage I shouted, "If you touch me again I will kill you." I laugh when I think about it now, as a skinny 14-year-old I couldn't have slapped him, never mind killed him.

Next day at school I was summoned to the headmaster's office and told in no uncertain terms I must never talk to Carol again, it turned out her dad had been up to the school that morning and told the headmaster that under no circumstances must Carol talk to any boys. In a mixed school that was impossible especially as she was a rebel and her dad didn't know, it made the whole episode a joke, so I had been given a smack round the ear for nothing. The laughable thing about the situation is on the day she said she would be my girl on that very evening she also arranged to go out with someone else. I learned of this about a week later from a lad who was in the same class as me and also lived in my road, at this time I was really hurt seeing as it was my first real puppy love.

MORNING DEW

My friend Duggie had cousins that lived in Polesworth, Staffordshire. We all went there on our bikes to look round the place, it was very nice, and on the way back we stopped at Tamworth where there was an open air swimming pool in the park – we all liked that, swimming in the open air. Some time later my other friend John suggested that we go to Polesworth camping for a few nights. John brought a loaf and a block of butter. I got a jar of jam, packet of tea and a bag of sugar just for the two of us. There was one little draw back, we hadn't got a tent! What I had was a towel, Johnny had a mac nothing else, to say we were not prepared is an understatement. It was warm on our bikes and off we went.

It was great fun cycling to Polesworth, we went through Tamworth and found a nice spot where some of the local lads swam. We were asked many times, "Do you come from Brum?" (in those days they didn't see many Brummies). One boy said, "Are you camping here?" "Yes," we replied. "Watch out for the farmer, he doesn't like people on his land, we always swim here in the basin, he catches us sometimes and gives us a clip round the ear," he then said, "Where is your tent? You will be cold by the river." "We will be OK, I'll light a fire," I replied. "Don't forget about the farmer, if he catches you with a fire you really will be for it – is that all the food you have?" he asked. "We've eaten half the loaf, so we still have half the loaf left and butter." "You can't survive on just that," he commented, then John reminded me we had jam as well. "That's still not enough, would you like me to bring you some eggs back later?" He shouted as he walked away, "I'll be back in about an hour." "We have no money," I shouted to him. "You don't need any, I know where they are free range, I know where the chickens lay them," he shouted.

About an hour and a half later he returned with four eggs, how wonderful to live in the countryside and get free food like that, one would never go hungry. We thanked him and said how kind he was, "I'll see you tomorrow," he said. "If you want any more eggs I'll get them for you." He shouted "bye" as he crossed the field. We gathered up as much firewood as we could to light the fire and got a real good fire going. Out came the frying pan, and with butter melted in the pan I cooked two of the eggs. I felt really good, and with two pieces of butter we made egg sandwiches, "We will have to come camping again, John," I said. "Yeah," replied John, "this is great ain't it, Dave?" I carefully placed the other two eggs in with the rest of the bread so they wouldn't get broken. "We'll have the other two eggs for breakfast," John said, so we saved those two eggs even though we were still hungry.

We decided to have a swim in the river after we had eaten, and we had a great time playing with the local boys. After swimming and drying ourselves on the towel it was so wet we lay by the fire, tried to put the mac over both of us and the soaking wet towel on top of the mac. Fire going, all seemed good, we fell asleep, then the worst of the nightmares started – I woke up shivering, wet and very cold, the fire had gone out; we didn't know mist from the river would soak everything. Trying to light the fire was almost impossible, everything was wet. We finally got the fire going again and as we got warm we fell asleep. Early in the morning a white mist was everywhere, the sun started to shine, John said, "I'm going in for a swim. I lit the camping stove and made two cups of tea with water from the river, I drank my tea but Jonny left his to cool down. "I will cook those two eggs after we have had a swim," I said to Johnny. We were enjoying ourselves so much we didn't notice what was going on around us. Johnny suddenly said, "I'm hungry, I'll cook those two eggs, Dave." "OK, John," I said, "give me a shout when you've cooked them."

As he climbed up the bank he gave out an almighty shout, "OH NO! Dave, come and look at this, the cows have eaten all our food and trodden all over our cooking equipment." I laughed, "Oh yeah," I said, "pull the other one." "No, Dave, it's true – come and have a look." To my surprise he was right, they had eaten all our food, they had trodden on the frying pan, ruined the primus stove, so we had no food or equipment. Johnny was so angry he threw everything into the river, so the great outdoor explorers were beaten after only one night.

We cycled to Tamworth Park to the open air pool, another warm day. We lay on the grass and dozed off for a short while, lay in the sun for a little longer, then cycled home. My bed was such a wonderful and welcome sight. I slept like a log, next morning back to normal. So if ever you go camping by a river don't be stupid like we were. Take a tent, better still stay in a hotel, but we never had any money so we made the best of what we had.

Enjoying the great outdoors without a tent

MY DAD

My dad worked at the Metropolitan Carriage And Wagon Works. That factory was situated in the area of Saltley in Birmingham. He worked there all through the war years. Every night when he walked in from work he smelled of suds (suds was a liquid soap that was used to cool down the drills when Dad was drilling). All his clothes became very shiny. His flat cap was that shiny I could have skated on it. He wore that same cap until the day he retired. It hung in the hallway with his waistcoat and overcoat. Those items of clothing were retired the same day as Dad retired. They hung there until the day he no longer needed them, that was the day he died.

When he was a working man he drank very heavily. Before he went to bed he would count all his cigarettes that were left in the packet. He would count all his change and put it in separate piles of copper and silver. He even counted the nubs in his waistcoat pocket that he hung in the hallway. No matter how drunk he was he did this every time he took himself to bed.

I started to smoke at the age of thirteen, I took a nub out of his waistcoat pocket. When he got up he told me he knew I'd had a nub out of his pocket.

One Sunday afternoon he really was the worse for drink (more than he normally was) and he took himself to bed. I waited until he dropped off into a deep sleep then I woke him and asked him if could have next week's pocket money. He said, "Take a shilling off the shelf," which was over the gas fire.

So the next Saturday afternoon I thought I would try the same trick again. He again was the worse for drink. So I waited until I thought he'd got into a deep sleep. I shook him and was shouting down his ear, "Dad, Dad, can I have my next week's pocket money this week and I won't have my pocket money for next week?" To my surprise he jumped out of bed and said, "You think I'm stupid, you came that last week," and he threw me out of the bedroom and said, "don't you ever wake me again when I'm asleep!" No matter how drunk he was, when it came to his money and cigarettes he always knew exactly how much money he had and how many cigarettes.

PAWN SHOP

Once a week my mom took whatever she could to the pawn shop, sometimes she would get 2/6d sometimes 1/6d, sometimes only 6d. Once or twice when I took some items of clothing they wouldn't give me anything on them. This pawn shop was in Wyndhurst Road, Stechford, by the Atlas picture house. I hated going to this shop, it smelt funny, it was dark and dismal. My mom had to pawn her wedding ring one day, they gave her 10/6 on it; that broke her heart, she never ever got it back. Many years later she bought herself a new ring. If it wasn't for that pawn shop I would have gone hungry more than once, so I suppose I mustn't knock it too much, they even later on in my life laid on a special bus to take people to that pawn shop. It isn't there any more but I'm sure people still need them. It was always called nunkies in our house, never the pawn shop.

As I was approaching the age of 15 years old I bought a lovely blue suit on the "glad and sorry" – I paid 1/6 every week, I earned this money by running errands. My mom of course had to make believe she was buying it for me. It was the first suit I had ever owned, and I only wore it on special occasions. As I didn't have a wardrobe in my bedroom, I had a picture rail running all around the room about eighteen inches from the ceiling, and I used to hang my suit with a coat hanger on the picture rail. I loved that suit. One afternoon I went to put it on (for what occasion I can't remember), only to find it wasn't there. Mother had been not very well off that month, she had pawned my suit two weeks before and, can you believe it, I hadn't missed it hanging on the wall and all that was in my bedroom was a bed.

MOM'S CAKE STAND

Off our kitchen was a walk-in pantry, in here was a concrete slab over the gas meter – this was called a cold slab, the purpose of this was to keep the meat and various foods cold as we didn't possess a fridge in those days, but there again not many people did. On the right-hand wall was the electric meter, on the left-hand wall were three wooden shelves one above the other. On the top shelf was a glass with Mom's false teeth in; here they stayed until she no longer needed them, even though she hadn't worn them for over forty years. On the other end of the top shelf was a cream cake stand that was purchased from Woolworths for six pence, long before the day I was born. It was used rarely in our house but it was used every Christmas Day and put on the table in the living room at tea time. Mom told me that when she bought that cake stand that all the items that Woolworths sold at that time cost 6d (six pence). This cake stand was Mom's pride and joy, I do remember her lending that cake stand out a couple of times to her friend Lizzie for birthday parties. It did get chipped on the underside which upset Mom quite a bit, none of us children were ever allowed to wash or carry that cake stand. (I am very proud to say I now own that very cake stand.)

I walked into the living one afternoon after school had ended for the day. To my surprise the table was laid with fruit, sandwiches, jelly and Mom's wonderful cake stand in the middle of the table with a cake on it. I was excited I can tell you, I hadn't a clue what was going on, not a soul to be seen then in walked my sister Doreen with her fella or as Doreen put it "her chap", my mom and other people as well. It turned out Doreen had been up to Birmingham Register Office in the city centre and got herself married. I was glad she was married, it meant I was going to eat all those nice things on the table, it was a rare treat. I knew nothing about the wedding until that very afternoon. It was a lovely surprise.

MY MOM'S DEAR FRIEND RITA HILL

A very close friend of my mother's was Rita Hill, and I'm pleased to say still to this day a friend of mine, her sister Ann, was a friend of my sister Janet. Rita lived in Swancote Road, we lived in Plowden Road, and our house was just across the road from Rita's house. Rita was still at school at that time, when she was supposed to be there she would sneak back and go to our house, walk in the back kitchen and shout, "I've come to wash up for you, Pross." She always called Mom "Pross". Mom loved Rita and always referred to her as "our Rita" like she was her daughter.

Rita, like myself, loves the past, and from our childhood days she has one memory that I think she could do without – our chicken Lonesome, yes it chased her up the line post, Rita was shouting, "Pross, Pross, the chicken's biting me." We were reminiscing about this on the 6th of August 2009; we were having a laugh about those days. She told me all these things which is how I come to know about them. As well as her sister, Ann, she also has a brother named Barry and we all played together from time to time. Happy days, eh Rita. I'm glad you are still my friend.

SHOPS REMEMBERED

My first recollection I have of our fish and chip shop was paying 3d (three pence), then 4d, then they went to 6d and stayed that price for a very long time. I can still see in my mind's eye those fryers, they were in the style that they had in the 1930s – Art Deco style. The mirrors on the back of the fryers which were situated against the back wall, opposite the counter where they served the customers, had a chrome edge all round, they looked like an opened fan; the outer mirrors were plain, the middle mirror was green with a picture of an old sailing ship with sails on it. I remember it so well because I admired it so much, I used to stare at it and study the art form, I just loved the shape of the whole fryer. The owner always asked if you had brought your own newspaper to wrap your own fish and chips in. I've seen those chips put straight on to the newspaper, I've even taken piles of newspaper to him myself, it never hurt us, in fact it was a pleasure to eat fish and chips straight out of the newspaper. I've eaten my share of newspaper ink.

Wrensons was the shop that is most vivid in my mind only because of the bacon slicer. That slicer used to fascinate me, the big wheel they turned to make the bed of the slicer move backwards and forwards. I stood and watched that machine doing its work while my mom was being served, that machine to me seemed to be dancing, I just loved that movement. On a white marble slab was a cheese cutter that really was fascinating to watch, a piece of wire was placed on top of a big block of cheese, and the manager (whose name was Oakley) would say to whoever he was serving the cheese, "Is that too big or is it all right?" If it was OK he pushed down on the wire with no effort at all, the wire did a perfect cut; it was then wrapped in greaseproof paper, very neatly wrapped.

Presentation in those days showed pride, slabs of butter were wrapped up in the same way as the cheese. When Mom bought

2oz of tea it was put in a blue cone-shaped bag; the sugar was also weighed and put in a blue bag and they folded the bags very expertly so the contents would not fall out.

The front window of the shop was big with two handles at the bottom of it so the window could be slid upwards. Behind the window was a large marble slab, bacon was laid on it in rows. In the summer when it was warm that window was opened – talk about health and safety, can you imagine all the dust and the flies landing on that bacon and who knows what else. Trouble was in those times there weren't any fridges, it's hard to imagine now.

In our two rows of shops were Stockton the newsagent, Holidays the butchers, and next to the butchers was a children's clothes shop The Walkin which was originally a fancy goods shop, Wrensons groceries, Braggs bread and cooked meats, Tranters hairdressers, Wilkes a grocery shop, Goldings Chemist, the Post Office, Browns the greengrocers then the Co-op. butchers and Co-op Groceries. On the opposite side of the road was Lathems haberdashery, the butchers, Hunts radio and bicycle shop, Saxons men's clothes shop, Paynes shoe repairers, fish and chip shop, Turners seed merchants, Carmichaels faggot and peas shop, Suches hardware shop and The Glebe public house.

Across the main road there were several more shops whose names do not come to mind apart from Ted Haynes, Stanley James, Vernons Gowns, Taberers newsagents, a shoe shop and butchers.

DISRESPECTFUL CHILDREN

As I grew up with my three sisters there was a word I learned to use that was used very frequently in our house, I must admit if I could change it I surely would and that word was “rotten”.

As the girls came home from school at dinner time, when they walked in the house from the backyard into the kitchen if what they saw for dinner was not to their liking they would say something like, “What’s this rotten stuff? I don’t want it, I don’t rotten like it, we had this rotten stuff last week, I told you I didn’t like this rotten stuff last rotten time.” Mother would say, “Stop using that word rotten.” Their reply would be, “Well you know I don’t rotten like it.” As I got older I automatically started to use it, it became normal speech in our house going something like this, “What’s for dinner, Mom, not rotten stew I hope?” We rarely had puddings in the week, I would ask after dinner, “Is there any pudding?” When I heard the word “yes” I got excited, “Cor, what is it, Mom?” “Ball sago pudding,” she would reply. I hate that rotten stuff (and I still do!). “Well bloody well go without then,” and I did. My sisters loved it, I had to watch them eat it. I would be saying, “It’s not rotten fair, they got rotten pudding.” Mom would say, “Well serves you right, they have had your share.” All I would be saying was, “It’s not rotten fair, it’s not rotten fair.”

Mom I think got a little used to us talking like we did. The one time that really sticks in my mind I was in my teens, I think I was fourteen at the time. Mom must have had a bad day – that day I had been playing football in the horse road as Mom called it, she called me in for my tea it was 4.30 p.m. I remember, as I walked in I took one look at the dinner and said, “Stew! I’m rotten fed up of rotten stew.” Mom shouted at me saying, “And I’m rotten fed up of you saying rotten, now it’s got stop, if you say rotten one more time I will put this plate of dinner over your bloody head.” For some reason (I can’t remember now why) I turned to look at the fire or to throw something in it, while I was doing whatever it was, I said, in a very cheeky manner, “Oh yeah,” and as I turned back towards the table, Mom had picked up the plate of stew, tipped it over my head keeping her hand firmly pressing the plate to my head. It ran down the back of my head and down my neck over my face and all down the front of my shirt. She looked me square in the eyes and with a fierce look on her face she said, “Well?” I was so shocked at what she had done I remember saying, “It’s better on the plate, Mom.” “Let that be the last time you talk to me like that, you hear?” “Yes, Mom, I’m sorry,” I replied. I had to have a wash down as there was not enough pennies to put in the gas meter to heat the water for a bath. I also had to wash my shirt and dry it as it was the only shirt I possessed.

That was the last time I ever said that to my mom. My younger brother John told me he tried saying rotten to Mom because he had heard me say it, he said she gave him such a smack round his ear and told him she would not allow it anymore so he never did again. I never did that’s for sure.

MISDEMEANOURS

Fare dodging we did on the West Midlands buses and trains, we worked out a plan. When we got on the bus we went downstairs, when the conductor came to collect the fare we would get up from our seat and as the conductor was taking a fare we would walk past him. We never ever tried it when a lady conductor was on duty, they never seem to forget who's paid and who hasn't, men on the other hand didn't seem to be as dedicated. Then as though we were getting off they would take no notice who was walking past them, so upstairs we would run, they had to concentrate on giving the correct change as you did not have to have the correct fare to pay as you do nowadays. The one thing I always did was to put bus tickets from past journeys into my top pocket and then the dodge we used was to take the appropriate coloured ticket from my pocket, hold it in my hand with my face pressed up the window, Trevor doing the same, with the ticket in full view so as the conductor walked up the aisle shouting, "Any fares please," it looked like we were looking out of the window innocently with our hand on the sill, as he walked past it looked like we had paid. We did this many times and we were never caught, as we were looking out of the window I would be saying things like, "That's the shop we went to," I could never think of anything else to say. Well it worked every time, we always had enough money to pay the fare just in case we were caught out.

Trevor and I used to chew lots of chewing gum. There was a machine on our Post Office wall that gave out a free packet every fourth turn of the knob. We tried many times to fiddle that machine by putting chewing gum on the back of the penny to make it stick so the penny would not go into the machine – but it never worked. Every packet had four pieces of sugar-coated gum inside it, if we only had one penny between us we would buy a packet and have two pieces each. We always shared and looked after each other, we never ever fell out that I can remember. That same Post Office had a cigarette machine outside of the shop and a milk machine; the milk machine held, what was then new, cardboard cartons with a pint of milk inside them. When we put our sixpence in we found if we kicked the front of the machine really hard we got two cartons of milk instead of one; after a few months that machine was so damaged it was taken away. In those days if a shop stayed open after five o'clock you were very lucky, that milk machine would have been a godsend to people working late. The cigarette machine suffered the same fate as the milk machine, both were taken away.

In those days the phone boxes had A and B buttons; if you couldn't get through to whoever you were calling, you pressed button B to have your money refunded. We found that by pushing a piece of rag up the return coin tray in the telephone box, when people would press button B to get their money back no coins would fall; punching, kicking and shaking and also putting their finger up the return tray compartment to see if the coins had got stuck, they would eventually give up. After they had gone we would go in with a piece of wire with a hook on the end, push it up the return slot, hook the rag pull it down and out would come the coins; myself I only did that once. I preferred to make my money by running errands for the neighbours. The reward for doing this was more satisfying to me.

A BIG THANK YOU

A big thank you to my mother whose love and devotion gave me the knowledge to overcome poverty and to show respect to rich and poor and to always have good manners. She has had to bring up seven children with never enough money to clothe, feed or to keep us warm most of the time. She was always there for her children. Many, many times she gave us her last pennies as we came first in her life. She could make sixpence go three days by buying bones from the butchers for the dog (which we hadn't got) with a pound of potatoes 1d or 2d and a pennyworth of carrots, would boil it all up, and with borrowed onions off her new friend Lizzie she got us through the week. My dad was no help at all, well most of the time. She lived like this well into her fifties; love and attention she gave us even after we got married. Most of her children she gave lodgings to when houses were very hard to get.

Thank you, Mother, we all love you very much.

Her children DONALD, KENNETH, KATHLEEN, DOREEN, JANET, DAVID and JOHN.

I wrote a poem for my brothers and sisters, and I've included it on the next page.

Of course in our lives each day we do things similar to the day before; this book only highlights some of the happenings in my life.

To my Brothers and Sisters

An uncommon surname have we
Prosser, it is and will always be.
Common values, common link,
As a family a true bonded link.
Seven of us grew up together,
Brothers and sisters no one can sever.
As a family there is no better.
Each of us was born unique,
None the same.
But what we share is the Prosser name,
Please always remember this.
Our wonderful Mother Dora
Blessed us all with a loving kiss.
Written for you all with love.

(Brother David Prosser, born 30th October 1943)

A POEM BY THE AUTHOR

Down our street when I was young
we played games all day long.
Hide and seek, tip cat poly, on the mop stick,
lots of games like that.
Football was my favourite game
I played this time and again.
I was poor but that didn't matter
when playing games I forgot the latter.
The only vehicles I used to see were horse-drawn carts,
no others I see.
So playing games in the street was not hard,
nothing ever stopped me not even those carts.
Those open spaces I used to know
were down my street where I still go.

My mom on a rare day out

EPILOGUE

In 1958 there were three terms for leaving school, EASTER, SUMMER AND CHRISTMAS. All my friends that I grew up with left in the Easter and Summer of 1958 and were working. I didn't leave till the Christmas 1958.

I found my last six-week school holidays very lonely, as this was the first time in my young life that I had no friends to be with. Day after day I struggled to think of things to do on my own. I still had three months of schooling left to do, this not only meant my friends would be at work but that they were no longer interested in playing in the street because they were now young working adults. Me, still a child at school, meant I hadn't grown up at that age like they are today – one week you are a child, the next week you become a young working adult.

Being on my own for those last three months after being with my friends from the age of five, doing so many things together for so many years, I found that very traumatic. I still wanted to play, they now just wished to act like grown-ups.

It's a shame to lose one's childhood overnight.

Trevor (left), author David (right).
Lifelong friends from the age of four
Reminiscing about our childhood